# WHAT TO DO WITH GRANDDADDY'S COINS

## A Beginner's Guide to Identifying, Valuing and Selling Old Coins

### By: Jeff Ambio

# WHAT TO DO WITH GRANDDADDY'S COINS

## A Beginner's Guide to Identifying, Valuing and Selling Old Coins

### By: Jeff Ambio

Copyright © 2010
ZYRUS PRESS INC.

Published by:
ZYRUS PRESS INC.
PO Box 17810, Irvine, CA 92623
Tel: (888) 622-7823 / Fax: (800) 215-9694
www.zyruspress.com
ISBN-13: 978-1-933990-24-8 (Paperback)
ISBN-10: 1-933990-24-4 (Paperback)

Coin images reproduced within this work, permission Bowers & Merena Auctions
Cover art by Bryan D. Stoughton
Cover photography by Brianna Cultice © Zyrus Press Inc.

Printed in the United States of America

# DEDICATION

To my son Tristan Drew. May God be with you always and guide you along the path of a successful and rewarding life.

Love always—Dad.

# ALSO BY JEFF AMBIO

*The Strategy Guide Series:*

*Collecting & Investing Strategies for United States Gold Coins*

*Collecting & Investing Strategies for Walking Liberty Half Dollars*

*Collecting & Investing Strategies for Barber Dimes*

*Additional Works:*

*A Handbook of 20th Century United States Gold Coins: 1907-1933*
By: David W. Akers
Revised and Expanded by: Jeff Ambio

*World's Greatest Mint Errors:*
*A Guide to the Most Spectacular Major Mint Errors*
By: Mike Byers
Edited by: Jeff Ambio

# TABLE OF CONTENTS

# ABOUT THE AUTHOR

Jeff Ambio holds a Bachelor of Arts in History from Cornell University and a Masters of Business Administration from Pepperdine University. Upon graduating from Cornell in 1998, Ambio decided to turn a life-long passion for coin collecting into a full-time career. Since that time, his career has developed into a successful and rewarding profession. Today, few other professional numismatists can lay claim to so prolific a career in so short a period of time. Ambio's numismatic resume reads like a directory of America's most prestigious rare coin auction houses and dealerships, and his writings provide collectors, investors and even other dealers with many of the tools and knowledge that they need to build significant collections and conduct successful businesses.

Ambio's first position as a professional numismatist was as a Cataloger and, later, Catalog Production Manager for the U.S. coin division of Heritage Numismatic Auctions (now Heritage Auction Galleries) in Dallas, Texas. During his tenure with Heritage, Jeff handled thousands of rare coins, produced dozens of catalogs and designed many of the marketing pieces published by the firm.

In 2003 and 2004, Ambio served as a Cataloger for Superior Galleries of Beverly Hills. He relocated to California in 2004 and accepted the position of Director of Numismatics for Bowers and Merena Auctions of Irvine. Jeff later served as Vice President of Numismatics for Rare Coin Wholesalers of Dana Point, California.

In addition to extensive cataloging and marketing experience, Jeff is a widely read numismatic author. His writings and articles are credited with ground-breaking work in the field and have appeared in numerous publications, including *Rare Coin Investment Trends*, *The Gobrecht Journal*, *Numismatic News* and *Coin World*.

Ambio is the author of the books *Collecting & Investing Strategies for United States Gold Coins, Collecting & Investing Strategies for Walking Liberty Half Dollars* and *Collecting & Investing Strategies for Barber Dimes* (part of the *Strategy Guide* series). He also revised and updated David W. Akers' classic book *A Handbook of 20th Century United States Gold Coins: 1907-1933* and edited Mike Byers' book *World's Greatest Mint Errors: A Guide to the Most Spectacular Major Mint Errors.*

Early in his career, Ambio's achievements as a numismatist were honored with a scholarship to attend the American Numismatic Association (ANA) Summer Seminar. In 2007, Jeff came full circle, this time returning to the ANA Summer Seminar as an instructor and originator of the course "Attributing United States Coins." He plans to teach classes on Walking Liberty Half Dollars and Silver Dollars at future sessions of the ANA Summer Seminar. In addition to several local and regional organizations, Jeff is a member of the ANA and the NLG.

In 2007, Ambio returned to his lakeside home in Texas, where he now works as a technical and marketing consultant for rare coin auction houses, dealerships, brokerage firms and private collectors/investors across the United States. His recent cataloging work has expanded to include United States currency as well as Ancient and World coins. Shortly after relocating to Texas, Jeff founded his own rare coin dealership – Ambio Rare Coins (ARC).

Jeff is the loving husband of Misty Renee and the proud father of one son, Tristan Drew. In his spare time, he enjoys fishing and studying European military history.

# PREFACE

I have been an avid coin collector for 26 years and a professional rare coin expert for more than a decade. During that time, I have discussed all aspects of rare coins and the numismatic market with thousands of individuals. Many of those people are seasoned veterans of the rare coin industry, but most are everyday people whose only link to coin collecting is the chance acquisition of a few old coins from granddaddy's sock drawer, cigar box, night stand or someplace similar. Indeed, the vast majority of conversations that I have had with people about rare coins have started something like this:

> Jeff, so-and-so told me that you work with rare coins. I have a few old coins that I got a couple of years ago from Granddaddy Pete (or Uncle Vic, Aunt Nell, etc.—fill in the blank with your own relative). Can you tell me what they are worth?

Of course, I am always willing to oblige, especially since the study of rare coins is not just a rewarding career for me, but also an enjoyable hobby and a source of great pleasure.

My willingness to help people determine the value of their old coins (to provide a free appraisal, if you will) also has a more serious purpose. I want them to avoid becoming lead actors or actresses in the most tragic, heartbreaking stories that I have ever heard about rare coins. They are the stories of lost opportunities, unfortunate mistakes and misplaced trust that always end with the forfeit of hundreds (if not thousands) of dollars worth of granddaddy's most cherished keepsakes.

The plot lines of these stories are frighteningly similar and usually follow one or more of the following four outlines:

1. Person finds or receives granddaddy's coins, takes them to the first jeweler/pawnbroker/dealer listed in the telephone book and sells them immediately without soliciting other offers or doing more research to determine the coins' true value. Weeks, months, or even years later, when talking

with other family members, surfing the Internet or having a chance conversation with a friend that they never knew collected coins, person begins to suspect or finds out conclusively that granddaddy's coins were really worth much more than the $500 that they received from the first appraisal.

2. Person finds or receives granddaddy's coins, discovers that they are "dirty" and cleans them with silver polish, baking soda, or some other kind of household cleaning agent. Person then takes granddaddy's coins to the first jeweler/pawnbroker/dealer and discovers that what was once $1,000 worth of coins has now been reduced to $400 because of their mistaken belief that the "shinier" a coin is, the more money it is worth.

3. Person finds or receives granddaddy's coins, believes that a Dime is a Dime is a Dime, a Quarter is a Quarter is a Quarter, etc. and takes them down to the bank and deposits the coins into their account as cash. Sometime later, when talking with other family members, surfing the Internet or having a chance conversation with a friend that they never knew collected coins, person begins to suspect or finds out conclusively that granddaddy's coins that they deposited into their bank account as cash were really worth much more money.

4. Person finds or receives granddaddy's coins but does not have the time or inclination to determine what they are worth at that point in time. Believing that granddaddy knew best, they put the coins into their own sock drawer, cigar box or night stand and vows to find out what they are worth at some point in the future. Sometime later, when talking with other family members, surfing the Internet or having a chance conversation with a friend that they never knew collected coins, person begins to suspect or finds out conclusively that granddaddy's coins are worth an appreciable amount of money. Returning to their hiding spot in the sock drawer, cigar box or night stand, they discover to their horror that granddaddy's coins are missing. A series of phone calls

and not-so-idle threats to family members and friends eventually results in the discovery that their husband, wife, son Johnny or brother-in-law Vito found granddaddy's coins one day and used them to buy fishing gear, make a few extra purchases at the food store, buy a pack of baseball cards and a soda or bet on the football game.

All of these plots lead to the same conclusion: the true value of granddaddy's coins is not realized and the once-fortunate heir is left with feelings of loss, regret and oftentimes even guilt.

The guilt is understandable since people faced with such an outcome cannot help but feel responsible for squandering part of granddaddy's estate. They often ask, "What should I have done differently?" It is my belief, however, that the blame for the squandering of granddaddy's coins lies not with the heir, but rather with a rare coin industry that has not provided adequate counsel to non-collectors who suddenly find themselves in possession of old coins.

You might be tempted to ask: "Why not speak with a number of rare coin dealers instead of selling granddaddy's coins to the first broker who made an offer?" A fair question, but what if the person did speak with three dealers and received buy offers of, say, $400, $450 and $600? Clearly, dealer #3 seems *more* honest than dealer #1 and dealer #2, but is he *truly* honest? Maybe granddaddy's coins are worth $1,200? In sum, how does someone determine exactly what granddaddy's coins are worth on their own?

But what about all of the books that have been published about rare coins over the years? Why not search for "rare coin books" on the Internet or inquire of a local bookseller? Surely a few dollars and a couple of hours spent educating oneself could have provided at least some sense of how much granddaddy's coins were worth. Another valid point, but as a seasoned rare coin expert and an author myself, I can honestly say that the vast majority of books written about rare coins are geared toward an advanced reader. The books are either specific to one type of coin or one aspect of the rare coin market, or they assume that the reader understands all of the terminology and vocabulary used by coin collectors and dealers. The Internet is also not much help, as much of the writing found there either falls into one of the aforementioned categories, is of dubious origin and, hence, credibility, or was written as a marketing piece by someone who is looking to buy as many coins as possible at the lowest possible prices. No, we still cannot blame the heir for not doing their homework before selling granddaddy's coins.

The only way in which the heir can be blamed for needlessly squandering granddaddy's coins is if they had access to a trustworthy individual—perhaps a family member or a close personal friend—who is an accomplished coin collector or dealer but failed to seek that person's counsel. As I have already stated, I routinely provide such counsel for family, friends and neighbors. But what about people who do not have access to a coin expert whom they can trust? Who do they turn to? Where do they go? What do they do with granddaddy's coins?

This, then, is the purpose of this book—to make the counsel that I provide to family and friends available to anyone and everyone who suddenly finds themselves with some old coins about which they have no knowledge. While I will continue to refer to these coins as "granddaddy's coins," where and/or from whom you got them makes little difference in the applicability of this book. If you have some old coins and want to find out 1) what they are worth and 2) how to get the most money for them, this book is for you. I hope it provides you with the information, resources and, above all, the self-confidence you need to prevent the gift of granddaddy's coins from turning into a family tragedy.

Jeff Ambio
Texas, December 2009

# ACKNOWLEDGEMENTS

Several firms and individuals were instrumental in the publication of this book. I owe a special debt of gratitude to my publisher **Bart Crane**, **Jessica Mullenfeld** and **Leila Benoun** at Zyrus Press. Bart and Jessica have been overly generous with their time and resources in the production of this book. Without their expertise and dedication, this project would never have been possible. Thank you, Bart and Jessica.

I would also like to acknowledge **Elaine Dinges**, **Ian Russell**, **Raeleen Endo**, **Karen Bridges**, **Ceilia Mullins**, **Ron Castro** and everyone at Bowers and Merena Auctions for furnishing many of the images used in this book. Karen and Ceilia, in particular, spent many hours taking and gathering the coin images and ensuring that they were in print-ready format. **Bryan Stoughton**, Creative Director for Bowers and Merena Auctions, also deserves special recognition for designing the cover.

# INTRODUCTION
## Early Retirement or 10 More Years on the Job?

Finding old coins in granddaddy's sock drawer or cigar box can be an exciting discovery. Our creator has blessed us with the ability to dream, and the discovery or other acquisition of coins is one of those times when imaginations can really run wild. Indeed, few other treasures more readily conjure images of wealth, prestige and status than rare coins. This is a holdover from past generations when only the most affluent and influential members of society could afford to collect coins. It matters little that, in the United States today, people from all walks of life have learned to appreciate coins as collectibles, investment vehicles or a little bit of both.

Your first experience holding granddaddy's coins will probably cause you to conjure some images of your own: that second honeymoon you and your spouse keep planning but never seem to find the money to take, a new car to replace the one that should have been retired five years ago, money for the kids' education or perhaps much-needed cash to pay down those medical bills that have been piling up for years. Before you quit the steady-paying job that you work so hard at or rush to the phone to call the travel agent we need to find out exactly what granddaddy's coins are worth.

Experience has taught me that the vast majority of coins that people find in granddaddy's sock drawer are worth only a few dollars. There are notable exceptions, of course, and the possibility that you found or were given a coin that is worth a significant amount of money is probably one of your primary motivations for purchasing and reading this book. So without further ado, let's begin the process of identifying granddaddy's coins and, more importantly, finding out approximately what they are worth.

# PART ONE

# TOOLS OF THE TRADE

# Chapter I
# Recommended Supplies

The process of identifying and valuing granddaddy's coins can be a lengthy one, especially if you are confronted with a large number of coins and/or a large selection of different coin types. The first step in this process—and in any process that you want to complete as quickly, efficiently and accurately as possible—is to gather the necessary supplies. Since these supplies will help to educate you about rare coins in general and provide you with the necessary tools to create a safe working environment for the coins, it is critical that you acquire these inexpensive products *before* you actually begin handling granddaddy's coins.

## *Rare Coin Books*

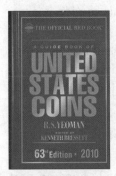

*A Guide Book of United States Coins (a.k.a. The Official Red Book) by R.S. Yeoman*

For the types of coins that you are most likely to find in granddaddy's sock drawer or cigar box, you need only acquire two books—in addition to the present reference, of course—that will aid in the identification and valuation process. The first is *A Guide Book of United States Coins* (a.k.a. *The Official Red Book*) by R.S. Yeoman. First published in 1946 with a cover date of 1947, the *Red Book* is released yearly in a new, updated edition. Principal differences from edition-to-edition are the inclusion of the past year's coins that were struck in the United States Mint and the updating of values provided for each coin listed in the book. In practice, the year-to-year pricing does not change all that much from one edition of the *Red Book* to the next, so you should not worry about using an edition that is a few years old. Remember, the purpose of this exercise is to determine if a particular coin is worth approximately $10 or approximately $1,000. The difference between a $9 and $10 value, or even a $975 or $1,000 price, is not going to affect how you proceed with the coin in question.

The *Red Book* is one of the most widely distributed books on rare coins in today's market, and obtaining a copy should prove to be an easy task. Online venues are a great place for obtaining a copy (see Appendix B at the end of this book for a partial list of websites for purchasing rare coin books and supplies), but most brick and mortar bookstores also carry the *Red Book*, as do many local coin shops. The *Red Book* comes in hardbound, spiral bound and combination formats, with the price varying from format-to-format. My personal preference is for the spiral bound version—it is usually a bit cheaper than the hardbound version and is much easier to work with since you can lay the book flat regardless of which page you are viewing at any point in time. This leaves your hands free to work with the coins themselves. Expect to pay between $10 and $20 for a new copy of *A Guide Book of United States Coins*.

The *Red Book* is organized in a neat, easy-to-use format with the coins grouped into three main categories:

1. <u>Colonial and Early Federal-Era Coinage</u>. This section is organized roughly chronologically, but it also groups the coins by association (i.e., Colonial issues authorized by the British Crown, privately minted coins, etc.). Included in this section are coins struck by or for use in the following entities:

   a. The original 13 colonies.

   b. A few additional British possessions in the New World.

   c. The French territories that eventually became part of the United States.

   d. The United States after the end of the Revolutionary War but before adoption of the United States Constitution.

   e. The original 13 states.

   f. The United States after adoption of the Constitution but before the United States Mint officially began striking coins.

2. <u>Regular-Issue United States Coinage</u>. Comprising the bulk of the *Red Book*, this section includes a listing of every type

of coin struck in the United States Mint either for use in circulation or for sale to collectors. The coins are arranged by denomination, or face value, from the Half Cent to the Twenty-Dollar gold piece. Within each denomination, the coins are then arranged chronologically from the oldest to the most recent. Additional sections listed after Twenty-Dollar gold pieces but still under the header of regular-issue United States coinage are:

    a.  Commemorative coins, which were struck to honor a person or event and were intended to be sold at a premium to collectors and other interested parties.

    b.  Proof and Mint Sets, which were also intended for sale at a premium to collectors and other interested parties.

    c.  Bullion coins, another category of coins struck for sale at a premium to collectors and investors who are interested in holding silver, gold and platinum in coin form.

3.  Additional Related Coinages. The final sections in the *Red Book* are arranged by group and address items in the following categories:

    a.  United States Pattern Coins, or coins that were made to test different designs, coinage metals, etc. These were never intended for use in general circulation.

    b.  Private and Territorial gold coinage. These pieces were struck by private minters in conjunction with various gold rushes that took place throughout United States history. For each gold rush, a dearth of regular-issue United States coinage and/or the lack of an official government Mint in the region explain the existence of these privately issued coins.

    c.  Privately Issued Tokens.

    d.  Coinage of the Confederate States of America.

    e.  Coinage for Hawaii, Puerto Rico and the Philippines under U.S. sovereignty.

     f.   Tokens issued by the United States government for use by settlers involved in Alaska's Matanuska Valley Colonization Project of the 1930s.

     g.   Error coins, or coins struck by the United States Mint that include some kind of mistake that occurred during the minting process.

     h.   American Arts Medals, which comprise a special series of gold medals struck by the United States Mint from 1980-1984.

The *Red Book* provides approximate values for each coin in a variety of grades, or levels of preservation. Therein lies the only significant shortcoming with the *Red Book* as far as its usefulness in identifying and valuing granddaddy's coins is concerned. The *Red Book* provides only brief, one or two-line descriptions to help determine the grade of your coins, and no pictures. For reasons that will be made clear in later chapters of this book, the grade of a coin plays a critical role in determining value in today's rare coin market. To overcome the *Red Book's* shortcomings in the area of determining grade, I suggest you acquire a companion reference: a picture-based grading guide that allows you to match your coin to a picture of another coin in the same grade. While I have provided you with brief verbal descriptions of the major grading tiers for United States coins (along with illustrations of Morgan Silver Dollars as examples) in Appendix C of this book, there is no substitute for having pictures with which to compare each type of granddaddy's coins. This is especially true if you are a newcomer to the world of rare coins and have little or no experience evaluating such pieces.

I recommend two coin grading guides as being particularly effective and easy to use: ***The Official American Numismatic Association Grading Standards for United States Coins*** by Kenneth Bressett (editor) and ***Photograde—Official Photographic Grading Guide for United States Coins*** by James F. Ruddy. Both books are organized similarly to the *Red Book* in that the coins are arranged first by denomination and then chronologically within each denomination. Both books also provide a wealth of supporting and background information on rare coins, coin grading and the rare coin market. Each book can be obtained on the Internet, from most brick and mortar bookstores and from many local coin shops. Expect to pay $10 to $20 for a copy of either reference.

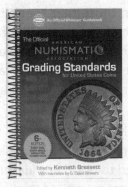 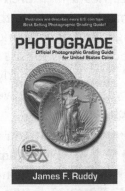

Above left: *The Official American Numismatic Association Grading Standards for United States Coins* by Kenneth Bressett (editor) Above right: *Photograde— Official Photographic Grading Guide for United States Coins* by James F. Ruddy

Whether you choose to use *The Official American Numismatic Association Grading Standards for United States Coins* or *Photograde*, you need to keep one point in mind. Both books are geared primarily toward grading coins that have seen commercial use and have acquired what rare coin experts refer to as wear. This should not be an impediment to your efforts, however, as most (if not all) of the coins that you find in granddaddy's sock drawer are likely to be worn from commercial use. These references will also help you to at least identify coins that are not worn, allowing you to separate them from the worn pieces so that they can be handled in the proper manner.

If there are any foreign coins in granddaddy's cache, neither the *Red Book* nor one of the aforementioned photographic grading guides are going to be of any use in helping you identify and value those pieces. World coins are much trickier to handle than U.S. coins, particularly since many display writing and other inscriptions in languages that might not be familiar to you. Of course, most European coins should be identifiable at least as to country of origin, the same also being true of coins from other countries that use the Latin or English alphabets.

I do not recommend purchasing a specialized book to identify and value any foreign coins in your possession that are dated 1900 or later, unless such pieces are struck in gold or another precious metal that carries a high premium. References for foreign coins tend to be much more costly than those that specialize in United States coinage. Additionally, most of the post-1900 foreign coins that granddaddy is likely to pass down to you will be worth no more than $5-$10. This is particularly true if granddaddy acquired the coins in everyday use while traveling overseas with the military, for business or on vacation.

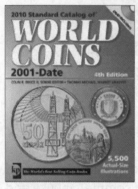

*Standard Catalog of World Coins*
*by Colin R. Bruce, II (senior editor)*

If you think there are some foreign gold pieces among granddaddy's coins, or if you feel the need to positively identify and value any other foreign pieces, the best general-ized reference that I can recommend on the subject is the **Standard Catalog of World Coins** by Colin R. Bruce, II (senior editor). This reference comes in five volumes that deal with world coins dated 1600-1700, 1701-1800, 1801-1900, 1901-2000 and 2001-date, respectively. Each volume is arranged alphabetically by country name, then usually by the face value of the coins (in ascending order from the low-est-value coin to the highest) and finally chronologically from the oldest coin to the newest. Be sure to check the date of the coin(s) you have before making a purchase to ensure that you purchase only those volumes that you need.

The *Standard Catalog of World Coins* is updated periodically, but there is no need for you to purchase the most recent edition in order to gain a rough idea of what granddaddy's foreign coins are worth. Just look for an edition that is no more than two or three years old. The volume that deals with foreign coins struck from 1901-2000 is the one that will probably be of interest to most readers, and it can be obtained from various Internet sellers as well as many brick and mortar bookstores. Expect to pay at least $35-$65 to obtain a copy of the most recent edition.

## *Other Recommended Supplies*

In addition to the reference *A Guide Book of United States Coins* and one of the aforementioned photographic grading guides for United States coins, there are only two other supplies that I would deem absolutely necessary as you begin to organize, identify and value granddaddy's coins. The first of these is some kind of protective holder for the coins. These range from inexpensive plastic flip-type sleeves to deluxe hard-plastic holders and cardboard presentation albums. Granddaddy may have taken the necessary steps to ensure the proper storage of his coins already, so you might not need these supplies. If you find the coins jostling around together in a plastic bag or scattered about on the bottom of granddaddy's sock drawer, however, plan on acquiring some kind of storage device to keep the coins from coming into contact with one another or potentially damaging surfaces such as a table top.

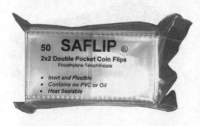

SAFLIP® 2x2 Double Pocket Coin Flips, an example of non-vinyl plastic flip-type holders for coins

To get started, I would acquire **non-vinyl, non-plastic flip-type holders**. They cost a bit more than a vinyl flip, but offer adequate protection for the price and the non-vinyl composition means that they are relatively safe for long-term storage. (Avoid plastic flips made with polyvinyl chloride—PVC—as coins stored in such flips for long periods of time will acquire an unsightly green film or spotting that can damage their surfaces irreparably and, thus, lower their value.) You can always purchase more sophisticated holders later on for those coins whose value and/or appeal warrant such treatment.

Non-plastic flip-type holders can be acquired at most local coin shops, some general hobby stores and through a wide array of Internet venues. They are offered in a variety of sizes and quantities, but in all cases the per-holder cost should be less than $1.

The final supply that you should invest in before you begin handling granddaddy's coins is a **soft, nonabrasive material** to line the table or other station where you will be working. The hard surfaces of wooden and metal tables can damage coins that are either dropped on them inadvertently or passed across them with the simple intent of moving a coin from point A to point B. While many jewelers, coin dealers and specialized websites sell velvet-lined trays for the purpose of safe inspection of coins, you need not invest the $15 or more required to obtain such an item. (Remember, we have yet to ascertain if any of granddaddy's coins are valuable enough to warrant such an investment.) Instead, I suggest purchasing a few pieces of **inexpensive velvet fabric** from a local fabric shop. Enough material to create a three or four-ply, 12-inch square cushion should be sufficient to line your workstation and create a safer environment in which to handle the coins. You should expect to pay less than $5/yard for this material.

## *Optional Supplies*

Unless your eyesight requires the aid of such a device, I would not invest in a magnifying glass or jeweler's loupe to make your initial identification and valuation of granddaddy's coins. A quick glance at the surfaces should suffice to identify most coins and determine approximate level of

An example of a flip-open loupe with 10x magnification

preservation and value. Bear in mind, also, that magnifying glasses and loupes can be costly (I have seen certain types and models with price tags of more than $150) and the investment is probably not justified if you end up determining that most of granddaddy's coins are worth only a few dollars.

If you are in the market for some kind of magnification device to view your coins, I recommend a **flip-open loupe with 10X magnification**. Weaker devices will not provide the necessary level of magnification, while anything greater than 10X is excessive in most instances. (I do not use a loupe with greater than 10X magnification when evaluating even some of the most expensive United States coins known to exist, and remember that I work with rare coins on a professional level every day.) A good middle-of-the-road loupe in the $20-$50 price range should serve you in good stead for many years. Look for such a device on coin supply websites, or ask your local coin dealer or jeweler if they either carry such items or if they can provide you with the name and contact information for their supplier(s).

It is also not necessary to invest in a special lamp or other kind of lighting device before making your initial assessment of grand-daddy's coins. Standard overhead lighting should be sufficient for your needs, and a reading or desk lamp that provides more concentrated light would be more than adequate.

## Recommended Supplies

1. *A Guide Book of United States Coins* (a.k.a. *The Official Red Book*) by R.S. Yeoman. Estimated Cost: $10-$20

2. *The Official American Numismatic Association Grading Standards for United States Coins* by Kenneth Bressett (editor) OR *Photograde — Official Photographic Grading Guide for United States Coins* by James F. Ruddy. Estimated Cost: $10-$20

3. *Non-Vinyl Plastic Flip-Type Coin Holders*. Estimated Cost: <$1 per holder.

4. *A Soft, Nonabrasive Material Such as Velvet Fabric*. Estimated Cost: <$5 per yard.

## Optional Supplies

1. *Standard Catalog of World Coins* by Colin R. Bruce, II (senior editor), multiple volumes. Estimated Cost: $35-$65+ (current edition of the 1901-2000 volume).

2. *Flip-Open Loupe with 10X Magnification*. Estimated Cost: $20-$50+

# PART TWO

# TRICKS OF THE TRADE

# Chapter II
# Handling Granddaddy's Coins

Now that you have acquired the necessary tools of the trade, you are ready to start learning the tricks of the trade. These tricks, or skills, will enable you to handle and store granddaddy's coins while preserving their value. First, let's ensure that you know how to touch, hold and work with coins without damaging their surfaces.

An example of holding a coin by the edge

Contrary to what many people believe, it is possible to handle rare and valuable coins with your bare hands. To do so safely, however, **you must only hold a coin by its edge**. There are natural oils in your skin that can discolor or otherwise harm the surfaces of a coin, thereby lowering its value. To prevent granddaddy's coins from suffering this fate, be careful that your fingers and hands do not come into contact with the coins' surfaces. Only touch the edge—the portion of a coin that rarely shows fingerprints or other forms of chemical damage to the detriment of the coin.

Our mouths also produce chemicals that can discolor or otherwise harm a coin's surfaces. As such, **make sure that you do not breathe directly onto the surface of a coin**. In the same vein, do not talk, chew or otherwise open and close your mouth in close proximity to granddaddy's coins. The saliva in our mouths can leave spots or other forms of discoloration on a coin's surfaces, thereby lowering its value.

Bear in mind that damage caused by oils in our skin or the saliva in our mouths may not be readily evident on a coin's surfaces. In other words, you might not know immediately that you have a problem with fingerprints or spotting on one or more of granddaddy's coins. It is just as disheartening, nonetheless, to find out that the bright, attractive coins you locked away a few months ago are now marred by fingerprints, spots or other unsightly features. By following these simple guidelines when handling granddaddy's coins, however, you will be taking the first critical step to safeguarding their value.

You might be tempted to use gloves and/or a protective facemask when handling granddaddy's coins in order to minimize your chances of causing chemical damage to the coins' surfaces. There is no harm in doing so (make sure, however, that the gloves are made out of a soft, non-abrasive material!), but a financial investment in such safety devices is probably not justified in this instance. Even professional rare coin experts often handle the most expensive coins with their bare hands. Knowledge is the key factor, and with the right guidelines you, too, can handle coins with confidence.

In addition to chemical damage caused by oils in our skin or the saliva in our mouths, granddaddy's coins are also subject to physical damage that can lower their value. **Be sure that you only handle granddaddy's coins over a soft, nonabrasive surface.** Should you accidentally drop a coin, therefore, it is much less likely to acquire scratches, nicks, dings or other forms of physical damage that could lower its value. Also, do not slide granddaddy's coins over a table or other hard surface as such handling can impart scratches or other detracting marks. The velvet fabric that you should have acquired after reading "Chapter I: Recommended Supplies" is ideal for making a tabletop or other workstation safe for handling coins. It is best that you place any coin that you are not presently handling either onto the velvet fabric or, better yet, into a proper coin holder.

One final word of advice is called for when handling granddaddy's coins, and it is actually better described as common sense than the sound advice of a seasoned rare coin expert. **Take your time and concentrate on the task at hand.** Like an expensive piece of china that you would never handle in a careless or reckless manner, granddaddy's coins also require patience, concentration and care. With the proper mindset and the right set of guidelines, identifying and valuing granddaddy's coins should be a relaxing and enjoyable experience.

## *Guidelines for Handling Granddaddy's Coins*

1. Only hold a coin by its edge.
2. Do not breathe directly onto the surface of a coin.
3. Only handle a coin over a soft, nonabrasive surface.
4. Take your time and concentrate on the task at hand.

# Chapter III
# Cleaning Granddaddy's Coins

The primary takeaway from this chapter is one that many people fail to learn. **DO NOT WIPE, BUFF, POLISH OR OTHERWISE ATTEMPT TO CLEAN ANY OF GRANDDADDY'S COINS**. The lesson is simple and to the point, yet it is so critical to preserving the value of granddaddy's coins that it bears repeating. So, once again, **DO NOT WIPE, BUFF, POLISH OR OTHERWISE ATTEMPT TO CLEAN ANY OF GRANDDADDY'S COINS**. As the Preface to this book makes clear, failure to learn this lesson is one of the primary reasons why many people are unable to achieve full market value when they decide to sell granddaddy's coins.

Improperly cleaning a coin, even with just a little bit of soap and water, will almost always cause *physical* damage to its surfaces. The damage is often on a microscopic level and may not be readily evident to the untrained eye. Rest assured, however, that improperly cleaning a coin—even with a mildly abrasive substance such as a bar of hand soap—will impart hairline-thin scratches to its surfaces. These scratches are actually called hairlines, and their effect on a coin's value can be catastrophic. Improperly cleaned coins are always worth significantly less than pieces that are left in their original state of preservation.

Notice that I have used the term "improperly cleaned" to warn you of the dangers in this area of handling granddaddy's coins. There are ways to properly clean a coin that can preserve or even enhance its value. I must stress, however, that only seasoned rare coin experts possess the tools, knowledge and experience to properly clean a coin. No matter how "dirty" or unattractive you think granddaddy's coins are, do not attempt to clean them. Sometimes what looks like "dirt" on the surface of a coin is actually natural patina, or toning, that can in fact enhance its value. In extreme cases natural patina can certainly lessen a coin's value. But in most cases it will not affect a coin's value one way or the other.

If you believe that cleaning could enhance the value of some or all of granddaddy's coins, consult a reputable coin dealer and ask them if they agree or disagree with your opinion. If they agree with your assessment, ask them to either clean the coin for you or to teach you how to properly clean the coin.

There is one other takeaway from this chapter, and it is closely related to the primary lesson about cleaning coins. **DO NOT ATTEMPT TO REPAIR GRANDDADDY'S COINS IN ANY WAY**. Some of granddaddy's coins might possess scratches, nicks, cuts, holes or other forms of damage that you suspect will lower their value when the time comes to sell. You are correct—such features always lower a coin's value—but attempts to plug a hole, smooth over a scratch or otherwise repair a coin will almost certainly lower its value even further. Even dealers and other experts usually refrain from trying to repair significantly damaged coins, being content with the value that the piece has in its present state of preservation.

## *Guidelines for Cleaning Granddaddy's Coins*

1. **DO NOT WIPE, BUFF, POLISH OR OTHERWISE ATTEMPT TO CLEAN ANY OF GRANDDADDY'S COINS.**

2. **DO NOT ATTEMPT TO REPAIR GRANDDADDY'S COINS IN ANY WAY.**

# Chapter IV
# Safeguarding Granddaddy's Coins

There are just two more skills you need to master before beginning the actual identification and valuation process, and they both concern protecting granddaddy's coins from damage that could lower their value when the time comes to sell.

## *Using the Proper Holders*

If granddaddy was an avid coin collector, chances are that he will already have taken the necessary steps to ensure that his coins are stored in the safest, most appropriate holders. The holders that granddaddy used might also be a critical component of their value and should not be separated from the coins. As such, **you should almost always leave the coins in granddaddy's original holders**. This is especially true for the following types of holders:

1. <u>Hard-Plastic Coin Holders</u>

Many of these holders, particularly those that are permanently sealed, contain information vital to the authenticity, level of preservation and value of the coins.

Hard-Plastic Coin Holder from PCGS

2. <u>Holders from an Official Government Mint</u>

Original Mint holders typically provide expert protection and ease of viewing for the coins in which they contain, and they can sometimes enhance the value of the coin(s) that they contain.

Examples of official United States government Mint coin holders

### 3.  Plastic or Paper-Wrapped Rolls

Be particularly mindful of original rolls that granddaddy might have obtained from a bank or other financial institution. These are sometimes worth a substantial premium.

$2 Nickel rolls, an example of paper-wrapped rolls

### 4.  Cardboard Coin Albums

For many of the coins that you are likely to find in granddaddy's sock drawer or safe deposit box, albums such as these offer protection, organization and ease of viewing.

*National Park Quarters Album*, an example of a cardboard coin album

You can always place granddaddy's coins into safer or more appropriate holders at a later date should you discover that they warrant such treatment.

There are types of holders that granddaddy may have obtained whose continued use I do not recommend. Many soft-plastic coin albums and holders sold during the mid-to-late 20th century contain polyvinyl chloride—PVC—which will damage the coins' surfaces over time. If granddaddy used holders such as these, or if you suspect that the plastic holders that he used contain PVC, remove the coins at once and place them into the **non-vinyl non-plastic flip-type holders** that I recommended purchasing in Chapter I of this book. Most of the non-vinyl plastic flip-type holders that I have seen contain two pockets, thereby allowing you to use only one flip to store two coins. **DO NOT place more than one coin into each pocket as coins can be damaged when they come into direct contact with one another**.

Your non-vinyl plastic flip-type holders will also come in handy if you found granddaddy's coins scattered around at the bottom of his sock drawer, grouped together in a cigar box or jostling around in a bag. Since you have to assume that at least some of granddad-dy's coins have appreciable value, I urge you to immediately place the coins into your non-vinyl plastic flip-type holders to safeguard them from further damage. You can always remove them from those holders if you discover that the coins are of minimal value.

## Storing the Coins

Even if you own a high-quality safe specifically designed for storing valuables and your home is protected by a professionally installed and/or monitored alarm system, **I do not recommend storing granddaddy's coins in your home**. In the event of a burglary, rest assured that old coins are going to be among the first items that thieves will take, especially since many people mistakenly believe that an old coin is a valuable coin. (See "Chapter IX: What Makes a Coin Valuable?" for a more detailed analysis of this point.) Safes can actually be a detriment in this regard as they offer a tempting target for burglars who are apt to assume, and usually rightly so, that if a home contains a safe, that safe is going to contain the owners' most valuable items.

There are, however, many reasons why people might still want or need to store granddaddy's coins in their home. Among the more frequently cited reasons for doing so are convenience and a desire to view, study or otherwise appreciate the coins on a regular basis. **If you do opt for long-term storage in your home, get an insurance policy to protect granddaddy's legacy**. This is particularly sound advice if granddaddy's coins are of sufficient monetary and/or sentimental value and replacing them would be too difficult or painful an undertaking. Your insurer will almost certainly provide you with prerequisites for honoring the policy. These are likely to include information on what kind of safe and alarm system to purchase, how to install and maintain them, steps to safeguard against fire, etc. The American Numismatic Association (ANA)—a non-profit organization located in Colorado Springs, Colorado that is dedicated to the advancement of numismatics—maintains contacts with underwriters for rare coin collections. Visit the organization's website, www.money.org, for more information.

Although not necessarily the most convenient storage medium, **the most secure place to keep granddaddy's coins is probably a bank safe deposit box**. This is my preferred choice because it removes the coins (and other valuables) from your home, making it less of a target for would-be-thieves. In this vein, it is also important to note that you should **never disclose the existence of granddaddy's coin to anyone except family members, friends or other critical persons such as a trusted lawyer or trust-fund manager**. Even so, it is a good idea to limit the number of people who know about granddaddy's coins only to those people who are absolutely necessary, and make sure the people you do tell follow your lead in this area. The more people who know about granddaddy's coins, the more likely the information will find its way to someone with the wrong intentions.

Regardless of where you choose to store granddaddy's coins, **make sure the environment is free of excessive moisture and heat**. Moisture and heat in sufficient quantity and intensity can react with a coin's surfaces in an adverse way, causing irreparable damage that will lower their value when the time comes to sell. Properly maintained safe deposit vaults in banks are climate controlled to protect clients' valuables. If you are storing granddaddy's coins in a safe within your home, make sure it is installed in a climate-controlled area. Additionally, do not place a home safe in an area that is likely to become flooded in the event of heavy rains or a ruptured water tank/pipe. And, of course, be sure to take all of the necessary measures to protect your entire home from damage and loss due to fire.

## *Guidelines for Safeguarding Granddaddy's Coins*

1. You should almost always leave the coins in granddaddy's original holders.

2. Use only non-vinyl plastic flip-type holders, and DO NOT place more than one coin into each pocket as coins can be damaged when they come into direct contact with one another.

3. I do not recommend storing granddaddy's coins in your home.

4. If you do opt for long-term storage in your home, get an insurance policy to protect granddaddy's legacy.

5. The most secure place to keep granddaddy's coins is probably a bank safe deposit box.

6. Never disclose the existence of granddaddy's coin to anyone except family members, friends or other critical persons such as a trusted lawyer or trust-fund manager.

7. Make sure the environment in which you store granddaddy's coins is free of excessive moisture and heat.

# PART THREE

# IDENTIFYING GRANDDADDY'S COINS

# Chapter V
# Taking Stock

With the proper supplies gathered and some critical skills mastered, you are now ready to begin working directly with granddaddy's coins. Your first step should be to pick a workstation that offers five crucial benefits:

1. Ample Work Space: Do not cramp yourself! Pick an area with plenty of work space so that you can spread the coins out and see exactly what you have with one quick, easy glance. Remember that you will also need space for books and other supplies, possibly even a desk lamp or other form of portable lighting. I recommend a large, flat surface area for your workstation such as a dining room table that is not used for other purposes on a daily basis.

2. Ample Lighting: Make sure that the area in which you choose to work is well lit. In my experience, sunlight shining in through a nearby window is inadequate for these purposes. For one thing, the light will not be concentrated in the specific area(s) in which it is needed—a drawback that will become more onerous when you start to evaluate the coins on a piece-by-piece basis. Sunlight also does not show coins in their best light (no pun intended), their surfaces often appearing dull and muted to the eye. In fact, I recommend closing all nearby shutters and blinds to block out the sun and going with either strong overhead lighting, preferably in conjunction with a more focused light source such as a desk or table-top lamp.

3. Personal Comfort: Depending upon the numbers of coins that you need to evaluate, the overall identification and valuation process could take a while. Be sure that you are comfortable in your workstation. Pick a comfortable chair that will provide your back with the proper support over a relatively long period of time. Make sure that you are also wearing comfortable clothes. Additionally, it is probably also

a good idea to have a drink and perhaps a snack or two in arm's reach. The more comfortable you are while working, the more readily you can focus your attention on the coins and ensure that the work you are doing is as accurate and efficient as possible.

4.  Personal Safety: Pick a work area in which you feel safe spreading out the coins and having them exposed for an extended period of time. Bank safe deposit vaults are not recommended unless they have viewing rooms that are secure, private and can be placed at your disposal for several hours at a time. If you are storing granddaddy's coins in a safe deposit box that does not offer favorable viewing options, plan a time when you can bring the coins home for a day or two. Try to ensure that you will be at home with the coins until you return them to the safe deposit box. Also try to avoid taking the coins out over a weekend unless you plan on working with them through at least Sunday evening. You do not want to take the coins out on Friday, finish evaluating them on Saturday afternoon and then have to keep them in the house for another whole day because your bank is closed on Sunday.

    Whether you are viewing granddaddy's coins in a bank vault or at home, do not pick a workstation that is or could potentially be in view of other people. Avoid tables near open windows or near doors that open to the outside of the bank or your home. And if you are working at home, also make sure that the coins are not within reach of young children or inquisitive pets that might be tempted to adopt one of granddaddy's coins as their next toy.

5.  Freedom from Undue Distractions: In the same vein, do not pick a high-trafficked area in which to work with granddaddy's coins. If your kitchen constantly has teenagers and their friends prowling around for food, do not pick the kitchen table as your workstation. Avoid rooms with a television that someone else is likely to turn on while you are working and, unless you are expecting an important call, try as much

as possible to let the answering machine do its job. Finally, do not pick a workstation that you think you might need for other purposes in a few hours. What if you cannot finish working with granddaddy's coins before you have to set the table for dinner? It would be a shame to have to pack everything up for the night only to have to spread it out again in the morning. Do not increase your level of stress by needlessly adding to your workload.

Once you've secured the ideal workstation, spread the coins out so that you can get a nice overview of exactly what goodies granddaddy left for you. This will enable you to begin to group the coins in broad categories for ease of identification and valuation.

## *U.S. or Foreign?*

The first criterion that I recommend using to break down granddaddy's coins into broad categories is country of origin. Chances are good that the majority of coins you have will have been struck in the United States Mint sometime between the establishment of that institution in 1792 and today. This is especially true if granddaddy did not spend too much time traveling overseas either for business or for pleasure. Coins struck in the United States Mint will display the inscription (or legend, to be more precise) UNITED STATES OF AMERICA, so spotting them should prove to be an easy task. There are a few types of coins that are collected alongside those that are struck in the United States Mint but are not products of the U.S. government. These do not display the legend UNITED STATES OF AMERICA, so you might mistake them for foreign coins in your initial assessment. This is perfectly acceptable. Remember, your primary goal at this stage of the process is just to separate those coins that are definitely products of the United States from those that are either positively from a foreign country or are not readily recognizable as to country of origin.

## *Gold, Silver, Nickel, Copper or Something Else?*

Next, I recommend that you break down the U.S. and foreign coins by metallic composition. This may be a more challenging task than the first one, especially for the foreign coins, but I would go with your gut instinct whenever you are at an impasse. Gold coins are almost always going to be some shade of yellow color. Silver pieces begin as white but will progress to various shades of deeper colors as the coins tone, or react with the chemical elements in the environment in which they are stored. Nickel coins can also look like silver to the untrained eye, but expect such pieces to be a deeper shade of gray when they are new. Copper or bronze coins are initially some shade of red in color that will deepen to more of a brown shade over time.

The foregoing is certainly not an exact science, and it does not take into account the myriad of additional metals and alloys that coins have been struck in over the centuries. Nonetheless, I do believe that this exercise has merit because, at the very least, it will help you to identify those coins that definitely carry some kind of premium based on their metallic composition. Due to the high intrinsic value of those precious metals, gold and silver coins almost always carry a premium (even if it is only minimal) in excess of their monetary value. You will want to set aside these pieces in a separate category from the nickel and copper/bronze coins, the later of which are unlikely to carry a premium based solely on their metallic composition.

To simplify your task as far as granddaddy's old U.S. coins are concerned, I am providing you with some general guidelines for determining metallic composition. These guidelines are based on the stated monetary value of the coins as well as the years in which they were struck.

1. Gold Coins: The United States Mint struck gold coins from 1795-1933, and then again from 1984-date. These coins carry one of the following monetary values:
    a. One Dollar ($1.00)
    b. Two-and-a-Half Dollars ($2.50)
    c. Three Dollars ($3.00)
    d. Four Dollars ($4.00)
    e. Five Dollars ($5.00)

    f.   Ten Dollars ($10.00)

    g.  Twenty Dollars ($20.00)

    h.  Fifty Dollars ($50.00)

Keep in mind that gold coins struck in the United States Mint beginning in 1984 were not intended for everyday commercial use but, rather, were produced for distribution to collectors and other interested parties at a price in excess of their stated monetary value.

2. Silver Coins: The United States Mint has been striking silver coins since 1792. Beginning in 1965, however, most silver coins struck in the United States Mint have not been intended for everyday commercial use but, rather, were produced for distribution to collectors and other interested parties at a price in excess of their stated monetary value. Monetary values for silver coins struck in the United States Mint include:

    a.  Three Cents ($0.03)

    b.  Five Cents ($0.05)

    c.  Ten Cents ($0.10)

    d.  Twenty Cents ($0.20)

    e.  Twenty-Five Cents ($0.25)

    f.   Fifty Cents ($0.50)

    g.  One Dollar ($1.00)

3. Nickel Coins: A relative latecomer to the family of coins struck in the United States Mint, our nation has only been striking such pieces since 1865. Monetary values for nickel coins struck in the United States Mint are:

    a.  Three Cents ($0.03)

    b.  Five Cents ($0.05)

4. Copper, Bronze and Related Coins: The most inexpensive coinage metal ever used in quantity by the United States Mint, copper and its related alloys have been used to strike coins by the federal government since 1792. Copper and related coins struck in the United States Mint and intended

for everyday commercial use come with only two monetary values:

a. Half Cent ($0.005)

b. Cent ($0.01)

## Is Anything Accompanying the Coins?

Now that you have broken down granddaddy's coins by country of origin and metallic composition (as far as possible for this initial assessment), I want you to create one additional group of materials at your workstation. This group will be comprised of any and all paperwork, holders or other materials that were with the coins when you found them in granddaddy's sock drawer. I cannot state this more emphatically: ***DO NOT DISCARD ANY PAPERS, HOLDERS OR OTHER ITEMS THAT GRANDDADDY HAS KEPT WITH THE COINS!*** There are two particularly important reasons for heeding my advice on this point:

1. Many old coin holders and albums themselves are worth a substantial premium to collectors. Sometimes such items bring a premium on their own, other times they enhance the premium of the coin(s) that they accompany. Be careful not to discard some of granddaddy's inheritance!

2. Paperwork and other supporting materials can provide clues as to where granddaddy obtained these coins, and the source of the coins is often a significant aid to determining their approximate value. So important is this point, in fact, that we will discuss it is much greater detail in a following chapter.

## *Taking Stock*

1. Choose a workstation that provides the following benefits:
   a. Ample work space
   b. Ample lighting
   c. Personal comfort
   d. Personal safety
   e. Freedom from undue distractions
2. U.S. or foreign? Group granddaddy's coins by country of origin.
3. Gold, silver, nickel, copper or something else? As far as possible, further subdivide granddaddy's coin by metallic composition.
4. ***DO NOT DISCARD ANY PAPERS, HOLDERS OR OTHER ITEMS THAT GRANDDADDY HAS KEPT WITH THE COINS!***

# Chapter VI
# What Are All Those Markings on Granddaddy's Coins, and What do They Mean?

Now that you have broken down granddaddy's coins into broad categories, it is time to positively identify each piece so that you can make accurate assessments of their value. To do so you will need to learn how to identify and interpret several key markings, or features on the coins' surfaces. Since the majority of coins that granddaddy is likely to have will be United States coins, and since such pieces share the same general characteristics, I will limit my discussion of key features to those that you will need to identify United States coinage. Many foreign coins also share these same features, especially those dating from the 19th, 20th and 21st centuries that have been produced by countries that use the same alphabet and numbering system of the United States.

1. Obverse: The front, or "heads" side of a coin. For most United States coins, the obverse is the side of the coin that bears the date.

2. Reverse: The back, or "tails" side of a coin. For most United States coins, the reverse is the side of the coin that bears the denomination.

3. Surfaces: The obverse and reverse of a coin.

4. Edge: The third side of a coin, and that which separates the obverse and reverse. Common edge types on United States coins are reeded, plain and lettered (with or without ornamental devices).

5. Rim: The border, often raised, around the obverse and reverse of a coin.

6. Design: The general motif of the coin, to include all markings and features that have been placed upon its surfaces.

7. <u>Device</u>: An element of a coin's design. In general usage among numismatists, the term device usually refers to the artistic elements of a coin's design and does not include such statutory elements as the date and mintmark. Devices are usually elements such as the portrait, eagle, the rays of the sun and a wreath.

8. <u>Field</u>: The portion of a coin's design where there are no devices or design elements.

9. <u>Legend</u>: Generally speaking, any inscription that appears on the surface of a coin. Many numismatists use the term "legend" to describe the inscription that identifies the country of origin for a specific coin. For almost all United States coins, the legend appears as UNITED STATES OF AMERICA, and it is usually (but not always!) present at or near the border on the reverse of the coin.

10. <u>Motto</u>: An inscription that forms part a coin's design. For United States coins, the term "motto" is often reserved for the inscriptions IN GOD WE TRUST and E PLURIBUS UNUM.

11. <u>Denomination</u>: The monetary value of a coin as assigned by the issuing government. For most United States coins, the denomination is present either at the lower-reverse border or in the center of the reverse. It can be expressed numerically (25 C., 50 C., for example) or in words (TWENTY CENTS, TWENTY D., etc.).

    *Note: Some of the earliest United States coins that date to the 1790s and early 1800s do not display a denomination on either the obverse or the reverse. On some of those coins, the denomination can be found on the edge. For others, the metallic composition and size of the coin alone were deemed sufficient to determine its monetary value at the time of issue.*

12. <u>Date</u>: The numerals on a coin that identify the year in which it was produced. For most United States coins, the date appears either on the obverse at the lower border or in the center of the reverse.

13. <u>Mintmark</u>: The small letter(s) that identify the mint in which a coin was struck. Mintmarks for United States coins can be found on either the obverse or the reverse, and are identified as follows:

    **C** — denotes coins struck in the Charlotte, North Carolina Mint from 1838-1861 (gold coins only)

    **CC** — denotes coins struck in the Carson City, Nevada Mint from 1870-1891

    **D (first use)** — denotes coins struck in the Dahlonega, Georgia Mint from 1838-1861 (gold coins only)

    **D (second use)** — denotes coins struck in the Denver, Colorado Mint from 1906-present

    **O** — denotes coins struck in the New Orleans, Louisiana Mint from 1838-1909

    **P** — denotes coins struck in the Philadelphia, Pennsylvania Mint from 1942-1945 (Nickel Five-Cent pieces only) and 1979-date

    **S** — denotes coins struck in the San Francisco, California Mint from 1854-date

    **W** — denotes coins struck in the West Point, New York Mint from 1984-date (non-circulating coins only; circulating coins struck in the West Point Mint bear the mintmark of the Philadelphia Mint, or else do not display a mintmark at all)

    **No Mintmark** — denotes United States coins struck in the Philadelphia Mint

14. <u>Designer's Initials</u>: The small letter(s) that identify the artist who is credited with designing a specific coin. Unlike mintmarks (for which they are often mistaken), designer's initials are usually very small, well concealed within the coin's design and may not be readily identifiable as to which letter(s) they represent.

For United States coins, the most critical features for identification and valuation purposes are usually the denomination, type, date and mintmark. Once you have identified and interpreted features such as these, you should be able to find the requisite listings for granddaddy's coins in any basic numismatic reference book such as *A Guide Book of United States Coins* by R.S. Yeoman and *The Official American Numismatic Association Grading Standards for United States Coins* by Kenneth Bressett (editor). Let's assume you have a 1911-S Barber Dime and you are working with the 2010 (63rd) edition of *A Guide Book of United States Coins*. Start by turning to the section of the book dealing with Dimes. If you know the coin is a Barber Dime, turn to the beginning of the Barber Dime section. If you do not know that the coin is a Barber Dime, that is alright since the *Guide Book* is arranged by date within each denomination. So, find the listing for the 1911-S Dime. Moving your finger along the row next to the 1911-S, you will come first to the mintage figure for that issue, or the number of examples struck. To the right of the mintage figure entry are a list of prices for the 1911-S ranked from the lowest grade to the highest. The grades themselves are listed at the top of each page and/or chart. To find the approximate value of your 1911-S Barber Dime, of course, you will need to determine the grade, which is best done using a reference such as *The Official American Numismatic Association Grading Standards for United States Coins*. That book, and other like it, are arranged similarly to the *Guide Book* and can generally be used in the same manner when looking up individual coins.

## *Identifying Granddaddy's Coins*

1.  Learn how to identify and interpret several key markings, or features on the coins' surfaces. For United States coins, pay special attention to the denomination, date and mintmark.

# Chapter VII
# United States Coins That
# Granddaddy Might Have Saved

Throughout my years as a professional numismatist, I have helped countless families and individuals identify, value and liquidate coins that they have received as an inheritance. My experience has shown that there are certain types of United States coins that are most likely to be found ratting around at the bottom of granddaddy's sock drawer or tucked away in his cigar box. Many of the older coins in this group could still be found in everyday use as late as the 1960s, thus explaining their relative availability during most of granddaddy's lifetime. Others have proven popular over the years as storehouses of value, works of art or both, thus explaining why granddaddy may have gone out of his way to include these pieces among his holdings even if he were not an avid coin collector.

The following images and fact lists are designed to help you quickly identify these widely encountered coin types and focus on key features for valuation purposes. In each case, the data provided is specific only to those coins that the Mint produced for everyday commercial use. Examples that are made solely for distribution to collectors sometimes vary in metallic composition, issuing Mint, etc.

### Indian Cent

**Years Issued:** 1859-1909
**Metallic Composition:** Copper-Nickel (1859-1864); Bronze (1864-1909)
**Mintmarks:** None—Philadelphia Mint; S—San Francisco Mint

Indian Cent, Obverse

Indian Cent, Reverse

**Mintmark Location:** Reverse—below the ribbon that binds the base of the wreath
**Special Considerations:** Although this type is commonly referred to as the Indian Cent, the obverse portrait is actually a representation of Liberty wearing a Native American headdress.

## Lincoln and Lincoln Bicentennial Program Cents

Lincoln Cent, Obverse            LIncoln Cent, Reverse

**Years Issued:** 1909-Date
**Metallic Composition:** Bronze (1909-1942; 1944-1982); Zinc-Plated Steel (1943); Copper-Plated Zinc (1982-Date)
**Mintmarks:** None—Philadelphia Mint; D—Denver Mint; S—San Francisco Mint
**Mintmark Location:** Obverse—in the field below the date
**Special Considerations:** Examples of this type that display the Lincoln Memorial as the reverse design, as well as those with special reverse design created under the Lincoln Bicentennial Program of 2009, are found in everyday commercial use. Even examples of the older Wheat Ears Reverse design are still sometimes encountered in circulation, as are the 1943 Steel Cents.

## Buffalo Nickel

Buffalo Nickel, Obverse            Buffalo Nickel, Reverse

**Years Issued:** 1913-1938
**Metallic Composition:** Nickel
**Mintmarks:** None—Philadelphia Mint; D—Denver Mint; S—San Francisco Mint
**Mintmark Location:** Reverse—at the rim below the denomination FIVE CENTS
**Special Considerations:** The date on the Buffalo Nickels is set very high relative to the other devices on the coin's surfaces, and it wore away quickly during every day use. As a result, many Buffalo Nickels that granddaddy saved may no longer display the date.

## Jefferson and Westward Journey Nickels

Jefferson Nickel, Obverse            Jefferson Nickel, Reverse

**Years Issued:** 1938-Date
**Metallic Composition:** Nickel (1938-1942; 1946-Date); Wartime Silver Alloy (1942-1945)
**Mintmarks:** None—Philadelphia Mint (1938-1942; 1946-1979); P—Philadelphia Mint (1942-1945; 1980-Date); D—Denver Mint; S—San Francisco Mint
**Mintmark Location:** Reverse—at the rim to the right of Monticello (1938-1942; 1946-1967); Obverse—at the rim below the date (1968-Date)
**Special Considerations:** With the exception of those pieces struck in the

Wartime Silver Alloy from 1942 through 1945, the Jefferson Nickel is the current circulating Five-Cent piece of the United States. Examples of even the oldest issues from the 1930s and 1940s can still be found in everyday use.

## Mercury Dime

Mercury Dime, Obverse          Mercury Dime, Reverse

**Years Issued:** 1916-1945
**Metallic Composition:** Silver
**Mintmarks:** None—Philadelphia Mint; D—Denver Mint; S—San Francisco Mint
**Mintmark Location:** Reverse—at the rim between the word ONE and the end of the olive branch
**Special Considerations:** This type is technically known as the Winged Liberty Head Dime, but it is commonly referred to as the Mercury Dime because the wings adorning Liberty's cap on the obverse are similar to those that are usually associated with the Roman god Mercury.

## Roosevelt Dime

Roosevelt Dime, Obverse          Roosevelt Dime, Reverse

**Years Issued:** 1946-Date
**Metallic Composition:** Silver (1946-1964); Copper-Nickel Clad (1965-Date)
**Mintmarks:** None—Philadelphia Mint (1946-1979); P—Philadelphia Mint (1980-Date); D—Denver Mint; S—San Francisco Mint
**Mintmark Location:** Reverse—in the field to the left of the base of the torch (1946-1964); Obverse—at the rim above the date (1965-Date)
**Special Considerations:** The Copper-Nickel Clad Roosevelt Dimes of 1965-Date are the current circulating Ten-Cent coins of the United States.

## Standing Liberty Quarter

Standing Liberty Quarter, Obverse          Standing Liberty Quarter, Reverse

**Years Issued:** 1916-1930
**Metallic Composition:** Silver
**Mintmarks:** None—Philadelphia Mint; D—Denver Mint; S—San Francisco Mint
**Mintmark Location:** Obverse—above the left side of the pedestal upon which the date is inscribed
**Special Considerations:** The date area was raised on Standing Liberty Quarters struck from 1916-1924, and the digits wore away relatively quickly in

circulation. Many of the older Standing Liberty Quarters that granddaddy saved may no longer display the date. Those pieces struck from 1925-1930, however, almost always retain the date no matter how much wear the coin acquired.

## *Washington, Statehood, U.S. Territories and National Parks Quarters*

Washington Quarter, Obverse    Washington Quarter, Reverse

**Years Issued:** 1932-Date
**Metallic Composition:** Silver (1932-1964); Copper-Nickel Clad (1965-Date)
**Mintmarks:** None—Philadelphia Mint (1932-1979); P—Philadelphia Mint (1980-Date); D—Denver Mint; S—San Francisco Mint
**Mintmark Location:** Reverse—in the field between the bottom of the wreath and the tops of the letters ER in QUARTER (1932-1964); Obverse—in the field to the right of the ribbon that binds the end of Washington's hair (1965-Date)
**Special Considerations:** The Copper-Nickel Clad Washington Quarters of 1965-Date (including the special Statehood, U.S. Territories and National Parks issues of 1999-2020) are the current circulating Twenty-Five Cent coins of the United States.

## *Walking Liberty Half Dollar*

Walking Liberty Half Dollar, Obverse    Walking Liberty Half Dollar, Reverse

**Years Issued:** 1916-1947
**Metallic Composition:** Silver
**Mintmarks:** None—Philadelphia Mint; D—Denver Mint; S—San Francisco Mint
**Mintmark Location:** Obverse—in the field below the motto IN GOD WE TRUST (1916-1917); Reverse—at the rim to the left of the rock upon which the eagle is walking (1917-1947)
**Special Considerations:** None

## Franklin Half Dollar

**Years Issued:** 1948-1963
**Metallic Composition:** Silver
**Mintmarks:** None—Philadelphia
Mint; D—Denver Mint; S—San
Francisco Mint

Franklin Half Dollar, Obverse

Franklin Half Dollar, Reverse

**Mintmark Location:** Reverse—in
the field above the middle of the Liberty Bell
**Special Considerations:** None

## Kennedy Half Dollar

**Years Issued:** 1964-Date
**Metallic Composition:** Silver
(1964); Silver Clad (1965-1970);
Copper-Nickel Clad (1971-Date)
**Mintmarks:** None—Philadelphia
Mint (1964-1979); P—Philadel-

Kennedy Half Dollar, Obverse

Kennedy Half Dollar, Reverse

phia Mint (1980-Date); D—Denver Mint; S—San Francisco Mint
**Mintmark Location:** Reverse—in the field below the eagle's left (facing) talon
(1964); Obverse—in the field above the middle of the date (1965-Date)
**Special Considerations:** Although rarely encountered in circulation, the Copper-Nickel Clad Kennedy Half Dollars of 1971-Date are the current Fifty-Cent
coins of the United States.

## Morgan Silver Dollar

**Years Issued:** 1878-1921
**Metallic Composition:** Silver
**Mintmarks:** None—Philadelphia
Mint; CC—Carson City Mint; D—
Denver Mint; O—New Orleans
Mint; S—San Francisco Mint

Morgan Silver Dollar, Obverse

Morgan Silver Dollar, Reverse

**Mintmark Location:** Reverse—in the field below the ribbon that binds the
base of the wreath and the tops of the letters DO in DOLLAR
**Special Considerations:** Morgan Silver Dollars were made in large quantities,
and most examples did not see active commercial use. While there are many
rare dates in this series, the Morgan Silver Dollar as a whole is a common coin
that was widely saved beginning in the late 19th century.

## GSA Morgan Silver Dollars

GSA Morgan Silver Dollar, Obverse    GSA Morgan Silver Dollar, Reverse

**Dates:** 1878-1893 (mostly)
**Metallic Composition:** Silver
**Mintmarks:** CC—Carson City Mint (mostly)
**Mintmark Location:** Reverse—in the field below the ribbon that binds the base of the wreath and the tops of the letters DO in DOLLAR

**Special Considerations:** When the Treasury Department halted distribution of Silver Dollars to the public in March of 1964, nearly 3 million Morgan Dollars were still on hand in federal vaults. Almost all of those coins had been struck in the Carson City Mint, and they were eventually sold to the general public in a series of mail-bid sales conducted by the General Services Administration (GSA) from 1972-1980. Most GSA Morgan Silver Dollars are Mint State, the coins encapsulated in black plastic holders within a black box that displays the Great Seal of the United States on the cover. A smaller number of examples were sold in soft plastic holders either because the coins were worn or because they display dark toning or some other real or perceived detraction.

## Peace Silver Dollar

Peace Silver Dollar, Obverse    Peace Silver Dollar, Reverse

**Years Issued:** 1921-1935
**Metallic Composition:** Silver
**Mintmarks:** None—Philadelphia Mint; D—Denver Mint; S—San Francisco Mint
**Mintmark Location:** Reverse—at the rim below the letter O in ONE

**Special Considerations:** Although much scarcer than Morgan Silver Dollars in an absolute sense, Peace Silver Dollars were also saved in relatively large numbers. Many issues are actually quite common by the standards of collectible U.S. coins.

## Eisenhower Dollar

Eisenhower Dollar, Obverse    Eisenhower Dollar, Reverse

**Years Issued:** 1971-1978
**Metallic Composition:** Copper-Nickel Clad
**Mintmarks:** None—Philadelphia Mint; D—Denver Mint
**Mintmark Location:** Obverse—in the field below Eisenhower's portrait

**Special Considerations:** The Eisenhower Dollar is often referred to as a "Silver Dollar." This is technically incorrect since only those pieces made for sale to collectors contain silver as part of the metallic composition. Pieces made for commercial use did not circulate to any great extent, but they can still be obtained from many local banks at face value.

## Anthony Dollar

**Years Issued:** 1979-1999
**Metallic Composition:** Copper-Nickel Clad
**Mintmarks:** P—Philadelphia Mint; D—Denver Mint; S—San Francisco Mint

Anthony Dollar, Obverse          Anthony Dollar, Reverse

**Mintmark Location:** Obverse—in the field above the edge of Anthony's left (facing) shoulder
**Special Considerations:** The Anthony Dollar was the first small-size Dollar coin issued by the United States Mint. It failed in circulation due to a similarity in size to the Washington Quarter, but examples can still be obtained from most local banks at face value. Certain government agencies (the U.S. Post Office and some local mass-transit organizations among them) continue to promote the use of Anthony Dollars in vending and other coin-operated machines.

## Sacagawea Dollar

**Years Issued:** 2000-Date
**Metallic Composition:** Copper and Manganese-Brass Alloy
**Mintmarks:** P—Philadelphia Mint; D—Denver Mint
**Mintmark Location:** Obverse— in the field below the date

Sacagawea Dollar, Obverse          Sacagawea Dollar, Reverse

**Special Considerations:** These so-called "Golden Dollars" actually contain no precious metal. Along with the Presidential Dollar, the Sacagawea Dollar is the current circulating Dollar coin of the United States, although examples are rarely encountered in everyday use. These coins are usually obtainable only from banks and certain government agencies, the latter of which promote the use of these pieces in vending and other coin-operated machines.

## *Presidential Dollar*

**Years Issued:** 2007-2016
**Metallic Composition:** Copper
and Manganese-Brass Alloy
**Mintmarks:** P—Philadelphia
Mint; D—Denver Mint
**Mintmark Location:** Edge—in-
cuse along with the date and mottos

Presidential Dollar, Obverse

Presidential Dollar, Reverse

**Special Considerations:** These so-called "Golden Dollars" actually contain no precious metal. Presidential Dollars are issued with four different designs each year commemorating the Presidents of the United States in the order that they served in office. Along with the Sacagawea Dollar, the Presidential Dollars are the current circulating Dollar coins of the United States, although examples are rarely encountered in everyday use. These coins are usually obtainable only from banks and certain government agencies, the latter of which promote the use of these pieces in vending and other coin-operated machines.

## *Modern United States Commemorative Coins*

**Years Issued:** 1982-Date
**Metallic Composition:** Varies
per Individual Coin/Set
**Mintmarks:** P—Philadelphia
Mint; D—Denver Mint; S—San
Francisco Mint; W—West Point Mint
**Mintmark Location:** Varies per Individual Coin

Commemorative Coin, Obverse

Commemorative Coin, Reverse

**Special Considerations:** Coins in this category are produced expressly for distribution to collectors, part of the proceeds from the coins' sales often going to offset the costs associated with holding a special event, restoring a historical landmark, etc. Commemorative coins are usually obtained directly from the Mint in the year of issue, but they can be acquired on the after market from dealers and other sources. The coins are usually offered either individually or as part of sets with other pieces of the same theme. Mint packaging varies, but many coins/sets were sold either in soft-plastic holders or hard-plastic cases, usually within a protective box or envelope.

## *Modern United States Proof Sets*

**Years Issued:** 1936-Date
**Metallic Composition:** Varies per Individual Coin/Set
**Mintmarks:** None—Philadelphia Mint; S—San Francisco Mint
**Mintmark Location:** Varies per Individual Coin
**Special Considerations:** These sets are usually comprised of one example of each circulating coin type produced by the United States Mint during the year in question, but they sometimes also include specially issued coins such as Commemoratives. The coins are struck with a special proof finish that is of much higher quality than the finish imparted on regular circulating coins. Additionally, some proof sets issued beginning in 1992 feature silver examples for the Dime, Quarter and Half Dollar. Proof Sets are usually obtained directly from the Mint in the year of issue, but they can be acquired on the after market from dealers and other sources. The original Mint packaging varies, but many sets were sold either in soft-plastic flips or hard-plastic holders, usually within a protective box or envelope.

United States Mint Proof Set, Obverse

United States Mint Proof Set, Reverse

United States Mint Silver Proof Set, Obverse

United States Mint Silver Proof Set, Reverse

U.S. Mint 50 State Quarters Silver Proof Set, Obverse

U.S. Mint 50 State Quarters Silver Proof Set, Reverse

## *Special Mint Sets*

**Years Issued:** 1965-1967
**Metallic Composition:** Varies per Individual Coin
**Mintmarks:** None
**Mintmark Location:** N/A
**Special Considerations:** These sets are comprised of one example of each circulating coin type produced by the United States Mint during the year in question. Special Mint Sets were issued in 1965-1967 in place of traditional Proof or Mint Sets, and they were originally obtainable directly from the United States Mint. They have since been available for purchase on the after market from dealers and other sources. The original Mint packaging consists of a hard plastic case to house the coins within a cardboard box.

Special Mint Set, Obverse          Special Mint Set, Reverse

## *Modern United States Mint Sets*

**Metallic Composition:** Varies per Individual Coin/Set
**Mintmarks:** None—Philadelphia Mint; P—Philadelphia Mint; D—Denver Mint; S—San Francisco Mint; W—West Point Mint
**Mintmark Location:** Varies per Individual Coin
**Special Considerations:** These sets are comprised of either one or two examples of each circulating coin issue produced by the United States Mint during the year in question. Mint Sets are usually obtained directly from the Mint in the year of issue, but they can be acquired on the aftermarket from dealers and other sources. The original Mint packaging varies, but many sets were sold either in cardboard or soft-plastic holders, usually within a protective envelope.

Modern United States Mint Set, Obverse          Modern United States Mint Set, Reverse

Modern United States Mint Set, Obverse

Modern United States Mint Set, Reverse

## *Silver American Eagle Bullion Coins*

Silver American Eagle Bullion Coin, Obverse

Silver American Eagle Bullion Coin, Reverse

**Years Issued:** 1986-Date
**Metallic Composition:** Silver
**Mintmarks:** None—Philadelphia Mint or West Point Mint; P—Philadelphia Mint; D—Denver Mint; S—San Francisco Mint; W—West Point Mint

**Mintmark Location:** Reverse—in the lower-left field below the olive branch
**Special Considerations:** These one-ounce silver bullion coins are produced on a yearly basis for collectors and investors who wish to have a holding in this precious metal. Both business strike and proof variants are struck, and they can be acquired either directly from the Mint or from dealers and other brokers.

## *Gold American Eagle Bullion Coins*

Gold American Eagle Bullion Coin, Obverse

Gold American Eagle Bullion Coin, Reverse

**Years Issued:** 1986-Date
**Metallic Composition:** Gold
**Mintmarks:** None—Philadelphia Mint; P—Philadelphia Mint; D—Denver Mint; S—San Francisco Mint; W—West Point Mint

**Mintmark Location:** Obverse—at the lower-right border below the date
**Special Considerations:** These gold bullion coins have been issued in tenth-ounce, quarter-ounce, half-ounce and one-ounce sizes. Both business strike and proof variants are struck, and they can be acquired either directly from the Mint or from dealers and other brokers.

## American Buffalo Gold Bullion Coins

**Years Issued:** 2006-Date
**Metallic Composition:** Gold
**Mintmarks:** None—West Point
Mint; W—West Point Mint
**Mintmark Location:** Obverse—
at the lower-left border below

American Buffalo Gold
Bullion Coin, Obverse

American Buffalo Gold
Bullion Coin, Reverse

the feathers at the back of the Native American's head
**Special Considerations:** These gold bullion coins have been issued in tenth-ounce, quarter-ounce, half-ounce and one-ounce sizes. Both business strike and proof variants are struck, and they can be acquired either directly from the Mint or from dealers and other brokers.

## First Spouse $10 Gold Bullion Coins

**Years Issued:** 2007-2016
**Metallic Composition:** Gold
**Mintmarks:** W—West Point Mint
**Mintmark Location:** Obverse—
in the lower-right field
**Special Considerations:** These

First Spouse $10 Gold
Bullion Coins, Obverse

First Spouse $10 Gold
Bullion Coins, Reverse

gold bullion coins are issued to commemorate the first spouses of the United States in the order that their spouse served as president. Both business strike and proof variants were struck, and they can be acquired either directly from the Mint or from dealers and other brokers.

## Platinum American Eagle Bullion Coins

**Years Issued:** 1997-Date
**Metallic Composition:** Platinum
**Mintmarks:** None—Philadelphia
Mint; W—West Point Mint
**Mintmark Location:** Reverse—in
the left or right field

Platinum American Eagle
Bullion Coin, Obverse

Platinum American Eagle
Bullion Coin, Reverse

**Special Considerations:** These platinum bullion coins have been issued in tenth-ounce, quarter-ounce, half-ounce and one-ounce sizes. Both business strike and proof variants are struck, and they can be acquired either directly from the Mint or from dealers and other brokers.

# Chapter VIII
# Counterfeit and Altered Coins

Counterfeit 1879-S Trade Dollar

Thanks to the widespread dissemination of numismatic knowledge and the advent of third-party certification, counterfeit, altered and other non-genuine coins have largely been driven from the rare coin market of the 21st century. Since granddaddy may have acquired many of his coins at a time when knowledge of counterfeit and altered coins was not as widespread as it is today, there is the possibility that some of those pieces may have found their way into his sock drawer, cigar box or other chosen hiding place. While I sincerely hope that this is not the case, you should familiarize yourself with the basic characteristics of these pieces and be on the lookout for some of the more widely distributed counterfeit and altered coins that still show up now and then in collections and other accumulations of old United States coins. By being wary of such pieces you will protect yourself from becoming over optimistic if it looks as though granddaddy might have left you a very valuable coin. He might have, but a little bit of caution in this regard will prevent you from writing large checks drawn off of counterfeit coins that are actually worth little, if any money.

## What Are Counterfeit Coins,
## and Why Were They Made?

Simply put, a counterfeit coin is a non-genuine coin. Counterfeit coins are made in various ways and for various reasons. Contemporary counterfeits are crude pieces, usually made in base metal, that were made to look like and circulate alongside genuine pieces of the same era. Contemporary counterfeits enjoy a dedicated following among some collectors, and some have even brought significant premiums when they change hands through auction or private treaty. These are not the kind of counterfeits that you are likely to encounter among granddaddy's coins, however, and they are also not the most dangerous forgeries. As previously stated, contemporary counterfeits are often crudely made, and even someone with little experience handling rare coins should be able to spot a contemporary counterfeit simply through side-by-side comparison with a genuine piece of the same design.

The types of counterfeits that you should be most concerned with when evaluating and identifying granddaddy's coins are those pieces that were made in later years for distribution to collectors and other interested parties. Sometimes these counterfeits were made with good intentions, such as to provide collectors with a replica of an extremely rare and valuable coin. Most of the time, however, counterfeits are made to deceive unwary collectors and trick them into paying large premiums for what looks like a rare and valuable coin. Sometimes the seller is the person who created the counterfeit for personal gain; other times they are an unwitting disseminator of someone else's forgery. Counterfeiters themselves have largely been driven from the market thanks to the efforts of third-party grading services such as PCGS and NGC, as well as professional numismatic organizations such as the American Numismatic Association (ANA) and the Professional Numismatists Guild (PNG).

## What is an Altered Coin?

An altered coin is a genuine piece that has had the date, mintmark or another feature changed, added or removed to simulate a different coin. In most cases, altered coins are created pass as (much) rarer coins. Unlike counterfeits, of which contemporary pieces that were made to pass alongside the circulating currency of the era are known to exist, altered coins are almost always the product of later generations of dealers and collectors.

Additionally, altered coins are almost always made for the purposes of deception, and some can be very difficult to distinguish from the genuine product. Remember, altered coins are made from genuine coins, so most of the design features will look real. The best way to spot an altered coin is to ask yourself the question, "What makes this coin so rare and valuable?" Is it because it bears a certain date, such as 1877 or 1893? If so, be sure to carefully scrutinize all four digits in the date for evidence of tampering. Is it because it was struck in a certain mint such as that in Carson City or San Francisco? If so, then you should spend a lot of time scrutinizing the mintmark and the surrounding area.

## Common Counterfeit and Altered Coins

Counterfeit and altered coins can be difficult to identify, even for seasoned rare coin experts with years of experience. The purpose of this section is not to make you an expert at identifying counterfeit and altered coins, but rather to make you aware of some of the most commonly encountered counterfeits in collections and other accumulations of old United States coins. If granddaddy has one of the coins on this list, I strongly suggest that you have it examined by a reputable dealer who will give you an honest and unbiased opinion as to the coin's authenticity. There are also independent third-party certification services to which you can send the coin for authentication purposes (if it has not been certified already). A small fee is involved, and you should also expect to pay shipping and insurance costs, but the piece of mind that comes from getting a truly unbiased opinion about a coin's authenticity is often worth the cost. Reputable dealers and auction houses can help you submit coins to third-party certification services such as PCGS and NGC.

In my experience, the following counterfeit and altered coins are those that are seen most often when searching through old-time collections and other accumulations of United States coins. This list is by no means exhaustive and there are many other counterfeit and altered coins known to exist from popular series such as the Walking Liberty Half Dollar and Morgan Silver Dollar.

1. <u>1877 Indian Cent</u>: I have seen both altered examples made from genuine Indian Cents of other dates and out-and-out counterfeits.

2. <u>1909-S Indian Cent</u>: Be particularly wary of an S mintmark added to a genuine 1909 Indian Cent.

3. <u>1909-S V.D.B. Lincoln Cent</u>: Many altered pieces are known with an S mintmark added to an example of the much more common 1909 V.D.B. Lincoln Cent.

4. <u>1914-D Lincoln Cent</u>: Sometimes altered by adding an S mintmark to a genuine 1914 Lincoln Cent.

5. <u>1922 No D Lincoln Cent</u>: I have seen some altered pieces where the D mintmark was removed from a genuine 1922-D Lincoln Cent.

6. <u>1943, 1943-D and 1943-S Copper Lincoln Cents</u>: Altered examples of these famous rarities abound, most of which have been made by plating or coloring genuine 1943-dated Steel Cents. Altered pieces such as these are easy to detect since Steel Cents will adhere to a magnet whereas authentic 1943 Copper Cents will not. Other altered examples that have been made from genuine 1948-dated Lincoln Cents are also known, and they can be more deceptive to the untrained eye.

7. <u>1955 Doubled Die Lincoln Cent</u>: Be wary of counterfeit pieces.

8. <u>1937-D Three-Legged Buffalo Nickel</u>: This popular and valuable Mint error is often forged by altering a genuine 1937-D Buffalo Nickel.

9. <u>1944 Jefferson Nickel</u>: A contemporary counterfeit is known without a large mintmark above the dome of Monticello on the reverse. Genuine 1944-dated Jefferson Nickels will display a large P, D or S mintmark on the reverse above the dome of Monticello.

10. <u>1916-D Mercury Dime</u>: Forgeries of this rare and valuable issue abound, and they are almost always alterations made by adding a D mintmark to a genuine 1916 Mercury Dime.

11. <u>1921 Mercury Dime</u>: Be wary of alterations made from genuine 1941 Mercury Dimes.

12. <u>1921-D Mercury Dime</u>: I have seen a few altered pieces created form genuine 1941-D Mercury Dimes.

13. <u>1926-S Mercury Dime</u>: Altered examples of this issue are not seen as often as those of the 1916-D, but they are also made by adding a false mintmark to a genuine Philadelphia Mint Mercury Dime of that year.

14. <u>1942/1 Mercury Dime</u>: Alterations are known with an extra digit 2 or 1 added to a genuine 1941 or 1942 Mercury Dime, respectively.

15. <u>1942/1-D Mercury Dime</u>: Alterations are known with an extra digit 2 or 1 added to a genuine 1941 or 1942 Mercury Dime, respectively.

16. <u>1982 No P Roosevelt Dime</u>: Alterations of this Mint error are known to exist where the P mintmark has been removed from a genuine 1982-P Roosevelt Dime.

17. <u>1916 Standing Liberty Quarter</u>: Be on the look out for 1917 Type I Standing Liberty Quarters that have been altered to simulate an example of the much rarer 1916 Standing Liberty Quarter.

18. <u>1932-D Washington Quarter</u>: Alterations abound on which a D mintmark has been added to a genuine 1932 Washington Quarter.

19. <u>1932-S Washington Quarter</u>: As with the 1932-D, the 1932-S is sometimes altered through the addition of a mintmark to a genuine 1932 Washington Quarter.

20. <u>1917-S Obverse Mintmark Walking Liberty Half Dollar</u>: Such pieces are not seen all that often, but altered 1917-S Obverse Mintmark Half Dollars are known to exist through the addition of an S mintmark to a genuine 1917 Walking Liberty Half.

21. <u>1921 Walking Liberty Half Dollar</u>: Sometimes altered from genuine 1941 Walking Liberty Half Dollars.

22. <u>1921-D Walking Liberty Half Dollar</u>: Be wary of altered examples made from genuine 1941-D Walking Liberty Half Dollars.

23. <u>1921-S Walking Liberty Half Dollar</u>: Alterations have been made by using a genuine 1941-S Walking Liberty Half Dollar as the host coin.

24. <u>1804 Draped Bust Silver Dollar</u>: Counterfeits of this, the "King of American Coins," are seen very often, many of which can be traced to a counterfeiter or counterfeiters in mainland China. Other counterfeit 1804 Dollars were made as replicas and sold as such to collectors seeking an affordable "example" of this rare, highly publicized issue.

25. <u>Counterfeit Trade Dollars, 1873-1885</u>: Many counterfeits are known, many of which are contemporary pieces that were made in the Orient to pass alongside genuine Trade Dollars in everyday commercial use. Some of the easier counterfeit Trade Dollars to spot are the 1879-S and the 1879-1885 issues. There was no genuine 1879-S Trade Dollars produced by the United States Mint, the 1879-1883 issues were struck solely in proof format for sale to collectors and the 1884 and 1885 are major numismatic rarities with only five and ten genuine examples known to exist, respectively.

26. <u>1893-S Morgan Silver Dollar</u>: This key-date issue is often counterfeited by adding an S mintmark to a genuine 1893 Morgan Silver Dollar.

27. <u>1928 Peace Silver Dollar</u>: Be on the look out for pieces that have been altered through the removal of the S mintmark from a genuine 1928-S Peace Silver Dollar.

28. <u>1934-S Peace Silver Dollar</u>: Genuine 1934 Peace Silver Dollars are sometimes altered through the addition of an S mintmark to simulate the more valuable 1934-S.

29. <u>Counterfeit Gold Coins</u>: Many counterfeit gold coins are known of the Liberty, Indian and Saint-Gaudens types. Due to the high intrinsic value of gold coins, I recommend having all uncertified gold coins authenticated by a reputable dealer or one of the leading third-party certification services.

# BRINGING IT ALL TOGETHER

# Building Your Coin List

## *The Importance of Your List*

Now that you have gathered the requisite tools, learned a few key terms and have begun to identify granddaddy's coins, you are probably asking yourself, "What do I do with all of this information that I am gathering?" The goal of this entire process (and the purpose for me writing this book, as well) is for you to learn as much about granddaddy's coins as possible. This information, in turn, will help you make an informed decision regarding whether you want to keep the coins, sell them or dispose of them in another way. The entire process of identifying, valuing and selling granddaddy's coins will be made much simpler if you pause once in a while to organize the information that you have gathered. Experience has taught me that building a list is the simplest and most efficient way to organize this information.

The purpose of this list is twofold. First, and most importantly, a list will help you organize all of the information you have gathered about granddaddy's coins in a neat, easy-to-read format. After all, many days, weeks, months or even years might pass between gathering the information about granddaddy's coins and deciding to sell some or all of the coins. If you are forced to set aside granddaddy's coins for a period of time, you need to be able to return to the task at hand as quickly and effortlessly as possible. A list will help make this possible.

Second, having a detailed list of granddaddy's coins and the information you have gathered about them will greatly simplify the process of selling the coins should you decide to do so at any point in time. In fact, many dealers and auction houses will insist that you send them a list of the coins after your initial contact so that they can learn the number and types of coins that you have.

## *Organizing Your List*

So how should you build this list? Should you type it or write it? What information needs to be included? How should it be organized? My answer to the first question is this: in stages. Build the list a few columns at a time so that you can concentrate on gathering only one or two sets of information at a time. In other words, if you are focused on identifying granddaddy's coins, focus on incorporating only this information into your list. Skip over grade, approximate value, buy offers, etc. The time to add that information to your list will present itself shortly.

My answer to the second question is this: whether you type or write your list is totally up to you. If you are skilled at using computer spreadsheet programs, by all means build your list using one of those programs. If you prefer that your list be handwritten on ordinary ruled paper, grab your pen or pencil and have at it. Remember, though, that building your list with the aid of a computer spreadsheet program provides many advantages, such as being able to remove certain portions of the information before showing the list to dealers and/or auctioneers.

Regarding the information that needs to be included, most of it will become evident as we work together to build your list. A few important pieces of information, however, need to be included right at the start of your list. First and foremost, title your list. This is particularly crucial if circumstances dictate that another family member finds your list alongside granddaddy coins after you have passed away. Don't leave them wondering what the list refers to and what information in includes. Second, and in the same vein, make sure to include the date or dates that you built the list. An old list will include old values, telling someone that the approximate prices of granddaddy's coins might have changed since the list was built. And finally, include your name on the list so that another family member will know who to contact should they need to clarify any of the information.

And finally, with regard to the organization of the list, I suggest ranking the coins first by country of origin, then by denomination beginning with the lowest face value coin and then by date. Within each denomination, rank the coins first by type, then by date and then, if applicable, by mintmark. This is the standard manner in which coin dealers and other professionals list their coins, and by using this method your list should be easy to follow for all readers.

## Starting Your List

Having just finished the chapters in this book dealing with indentifying granddaddy's coins, let's start building your list with this information. You will probably need only five columns to accurately convey the identity of each coin. For your convenience, I have included a sample list comprised only of these five columns on the following page:

## List of Granddaddy Glynn's Coins[1]

| Country | Denomination | Type | Date | Mintmark |
|---|---|---|---|---|
| United States | Cent | Indian | 1902 | None |
| United States | Dime | Seated Liberty | 1843 | O |
| United States | Half Dollar | Kennedy | 1996 | D |
| United States | Silver Dollar | Morgan | 1880 | None |
| United States | Eagle-$10 Gold | Indian | 1930 | S |
| United States | (5) Coins | Proof Set | 1986 | S |
| Great Britain | Penny | Queen Victoria | 1895 | None |

1=Prepared June-December 2009, by Jeff Ambio.

# PART FOUR

# VALUING GRANDDADDY'S COINS

# Chapter IX
# What Makes a Coin Valuable?

Now that you have identified granddaddy's coins, you are nearly ready to assign them approximate values that will help you determine when and how to sell the coins (if you should choose to do so). Before we begin this stage of the process, however, it would help if you understood some of the factors governing value in the rare coin market of the 21$^{st}$ century.

## *Age*

Contrary to popular belief, the age, or how old a coin is, has no affect upon its value. The date of a coin, of course, plays an important role in determining value, but a coin that was made 150 years ago is not necessarily worth more money than a coin that was produced 25 years ago just because it is 125 years older. Take for example the following comparison between two coins, both of which are examples of types that are among the most popular and widely collected ever produced in the United States Mint. In both cases, the prices reflect coins graded VF-20 and are drawn from the 2010 edition of the widely used price guide *A Guide Book of United States Coins* (a.k.a. *The Official Red Book*) by R.S. Yeoman.

1. <u>1879 Morgan Silver Dollar</u>: *Red Book* price in VF-20 = $22.
2. <u>1916-D Mercury Dime</u>: *Red Book* price in VF-20 = $4,200.

Clearly age does not determine value in the rare coin market, or else the older 1879 Morgan Silver Dollar would be worth more than the 1916-D Mercury Dime.

## *Rarity, or Supply*

The number of examples known to exist for a specific issue certainly plays an important role in determining a coin's value. The current supply of a certain coin is based on several factors, the easiest of which to discern is the number of pieces initially struck. Looking again at the 1879 Morgan Silver Dollar and the 1916-D

Mercury Dime, we see the following mintage figures as reported in the 2010 edition of the book *A Guide Book of United States Coins* by R.S. Yeoman:

1. <u>1879 Morgan Silver Dollar</u>: 14,806,000 pieces struck
2. <u>1916-D Mercury Dime</u>: 264,000 pieces struck

Obviously, the 1916-D Mercury Dime has always been a rarer coin than the 1879 Morgan Silver Dollar because far fewer examples were produced. The greater rarity, in turn, has resulted in the greater value attached to the 1916-D Mercury Dime.

Another factor affecting the current supply of a coin is distribution, or how the coins were used, stored or destroyed by the federal government, financial institutions and private citizens. Two examples will suffice to illustrate this concept. First, let's look at the 1877 and 1909-S Indian Cents. Both are low-mintage issues with 852,900 pieces and 309,000 pieces produced, respectively. In the grade of MS-63 BN, however, the 1877 is bid at $3,760 in the May 8, 2009 issue of *The Coin Dealer Newsletter: CDN Monthly Supplement*. Despite a lower mintage, however, the 1909-S in MS-63 BN is bid at "only" $900 in the same source. Why the seeming discrepancy? The 1877 was used more heavily in circulation than the 1909-S, and fewer examples were saved by the contemporary public. In fact, I estimate that approximately 95-110 examples of the 1909-S Indian Cent that grade MS-63 BN are known to exist. My estimate for the 1877 in the same grade is much lower at 45-55 coins.

A second example to illustrate this point is a comparison between the 1908-S and 1927-S Saint-Gaudens Double Eagles. In my revision to the 1988 book *A Handbook of 20th Century United States Gold Coins: 1907-1933* by David W. Akers, I estimate that 210-275 Mint State examples of the 1908-S have survived from a low mintage of just 22,000 pieces. The 1927-S was produced in much greater numbers—3,107,000 pieces, to be exact—but my estimate on the number of Mint State coins extant is only 120-140 pieces. The discrepancy here can be explained through distribution. The 1908-S was the first Saint-Gaudens Double Eagle struck in the San Francisco Mint, and a fair number of Mint State examples were saved as novelty items. By comparison, the Mint released few 1927-S Double Eagles into commercial channels, the majority of the mintage remaining in federal vaults until it was destroyed during the height of the Great Depression by order of President Franklin D. Roosevelt.

## Popularity, or Demand

Just having a low mintage and/or a poor rate of survival is not always sufficient to guarantee a strong price for many United States coins. Collectors, dealers and others have to want to pay a strong price for the coin. In other words, the coin must be sufficiently popular with a requisite level of demand in relation to its rarity to ensure a strong price in the market. Take for example the 1855-S Arrows Seated Liberty Quarter and the 1927-S Standing Liberty Quarter. Both have nearly identical mintage figures at 396,400 pieces and 396,000 coins, respectively. Yet in the popular grade of AU-50 the 2010 edition of the book *A Guide Book of United States Coins* by R.S. Yeoman provides a price of $700 for the 1855-S and $2,800 for the 1927-S. And this is despite the fact that the 1855-S is the rarer coin. PCGS and NGC—two of the leading third-party certification services in the rare coin market of the 21st century—have certified approximately 60 examples of the 1855-S Arrows Seated Liberty Quarter in all grades. The number of 1927-S Standing Liberty Quarters certified in all grades is much higher at more than 1,850 coins.

The Standing Liberty Quarter series of 1916-1930 is widely collected in today's market with many numismatists willing to pay a strong premium to obtain an example of the low-mintage 1927-S. The Seated Liberty Quarter series of 1838-1891, however, does not enjoy such demand. The result is that there are far fewer collectors looking for an example of the 1855-S.

## Grade, or Level of Preservation

The grade, or level of preservation of a coin plays a huge role in determining its value, especially in the United States rare coin market of the 21st century. United States coins are graded on a numeric scale from 1-70, each grading tier also being accompanied by a descriptive modifier such as Very Fine (for numeric grades of 20, 25, 30 and 35) and Extremely Fine (for numeric grades of 40 and 45). The higher the numeric grade, the better preserved and, hence, more desirable the coin. See Appendix C for a detailed grading chart.

The grade of a coin is such an integral part of its value that the price of two examples of the exact same issue might be separated by thousands of dollars depending on the individual grade of each piece. Some of the best illustrations of this phenomenon can be found in the ever-popular Morgan Silver Dollar series of 1878-1921. The prices for each of these coins are drawn from the 2010 edition of the book *A Guide Book of United States Coins* (*The Official Red Book*) by R.S. Yeoman.

1. <u>1886-O Morgan Silver Dollar</u>:
   i. *Red Book* price in VF-20 = $25
   ii. *Red Book* price in MS-65 = $225,000
2. <u>1892-S Morgan Silver Dollar</u>:
   i. *Red Book* price in VF-20 = $100
   ii. *Red Book* price in MS-65 = $192,500
3. <u>1895-O Morgan Silver Dollar</u>:
   i. *Red Book* price in VF-20 = $600
   ii. *Red Book* price in MS-65 = $225,000
4. <u>1901 Morgan Silver Dollar</u>:
   i. *Red Book* price in VF-20 = $50
   ii. *Red Book* price in MS-65 = $325,000

It is imperative that you make full use of grading guides such as *The Official American Numismatic Association Grading Standards for United States Coins* by Kenneth Bressett (editor) and *Photograde—Official Photographic Grading Guide for United States Coins* by James F. Ruddy to determine the grade (even if it only approximate) of granddaddy's coins after you have identified them. This is a critical step in the evaluation process that will prevent you from either undervaluing or overvaluing some of granddaddy's coins. Undervaluing is obviously dangerous lest you leave money on the table if and when you decide to sell. And the danger of overvaluing is that your hopes might be dashed if you are expecting to get a check for $200,000+ for one of granddaddy's coins and instead receive only $20 at the time of sale.

If you are having difficulty using one of the recommended grading guides, or if you are just not that confident with your ability to assign even approximate grades to the coins, have them evaluated by a trusted, reputable dealer. You can also consider submitting the coins to an independent third-party certification service to have grades assigned, but I would only take that step if you have already determined that the coins are of sufficient value to justify the costs associated with these services.

*Note: Please see "Chapter XIV: Appraisals and Third-Party Certification" for a detailed description of third-party certification as it pertains to the rare coin market of the 21st century.*

# Chapter X
# Consider the Source

There is actually a way that you can "cheat" to determine the approximate value of granddaddy's coins without having to spend a lot of time looking through grading and price guides. By evaluating where and when granddaddy acquired the coins, and then looking at how he stored them over the years, chances are good that you will be able to determine whether the coins are worth only a few dollars or potentially much more. While there is no real substitute for evaluating granddaddy's coins using standard numismatic references guides and/or consulting a reputable dealer, looking at the coins through granddaddy's eyes can still be a powerful tool, especially if you are having difficulty matching a particular coin to one of two pricing extremes.

## *Where Did Granddaddy Acquire the Coins?*

This question might be difficult if not impossible to answer, especially if granddaddy was very secretive about his coins and did not leave any written records concerning his acquisitions. If granddaddy shared his passion for coins with other family members, or if he left paperwork such as invoices and inventory lists with the coins (you did save all of the accompanying paperwork as I recommended in Chapter V, right?), it should be relatively easy to determine where, when and under what circumstances he obtained these coins. Chances are good that he acquired the coins through one of the following means:

1. Circulation: Granddaddy may have been an accumulator or only a casual collector, acquiring what he perceived to be interesting or valuable coins as he came across them in everyday use. If this was the source for most or all of his pieces, it is likely that granddaddy's coins are worth face value or a small premium over face value. This is especially true if granddaddy acquired most of his coins from circulation after the mid 1960s.

2. <u>Overseas Travel</u>: If granddaddy served in the military, he may have spent a considerable amount of time in the Far East. Or he may have traveled overseas for business or pleasure. If he brought any United States coins back home with him, especially from the Far East, chances are good that they will be examples of one of two types: 1) counterfeit or replica 1804 Draped Bust Silver Dollars; 2) counterfeit Trade Dollars dated 1873-1885. These coins have little, if any value attached to them.

    As an aside here, any foreign coins that granddaddy retrieved from circulation while overseas are likely to carry only a minimal premium over face value. Many such pieces do not carry a premium at all and are still worth only face value in their respective country of origin.

3. <u>Local and Regional Dealers, Auctions and Flea Markets</u>: Perhaps granddaddy was a little more serious about coin collecting and was willing to pay a premium to acquire pieces that he needed to complete a set or fulfill some other desire. If his source for the coins were local and regional dealers, auctions and/or flea markets, particularly those that did not specialize in rare coins, the individual pieces that he acquired are probably worth no more than a couple of hundred dollars, and probably significantly less.

4. <u>National Dealers and Auctions</u>: If granddaddy bought coins at this level, it is likely that he was paying a significant premium for the coins that he purchased. And provided that granddaddy was a knowledgeable coin buyer and was working with reputable dealers and auction houses, the chances are also good that his coins have either retained their value or have increased (perhaps dramatically) in price. At this level granddaddy can be classified as a serious collector, and he obviously went out of his way to find dealers and auctioneers that enjoyed strong reputations and had the ability to draw buyers and sellers from around the country.

5. <u>Inheritance</u>: It is always possible that granddaddy inherited some or all of these coins from his granddaddy. If so, the

category in which you should place his coins in terms of their potential value will depend greatly upon where and how his granddaddy acquired the coins. With this scenario it is important that you remain open to the option that granddaddy may have received some of the coins as an inheritance but then added to the collection himself.

I know of many families where granddaddy's gift of a few silver Dimes worth less than $1.00 each turned a grandson or granddaughter into a serious collector who has subsequently spent thousands of dollars assembling a world-class collection. (I myself would probably not be writing this book if my granddaddy had not given me a 1936-S Buffalo Nickel and a 1940 Mercury Dime when I was seven years old. Granddaddy had saved the coins from circulation when he was younger, and their combined value even now is less than $5, but they sparked a passion for coins that would eventually lead me to embark upon a long-term career as a professional numismatist.) The opposite scenario can also be true, of course, and I remember handling coins from a family where the father was a serious collector who travelled the globe in search of the rarest and finest coins that he could afford. The son who received the inheritance, on the other hand, added to his father's collection by purchasing mostly inexpensive coins from dealer junk boxes, local flea markets and the like.

## When Did Granddaddy Acquire the Coins?

As to the "when" of granddaddy's coin acquisitions, there are two major time frames with which you should be concerned.

1. Pre-1965: Prior to 1965, the United States Mint struck silver Dimes, Quarters and Half Dollars for use in everyday circulation. Additionally, coin collecting was nowhere near as popular a pastime as it is in the 21st century. The combination of these two factors meant that it was possible to find many older coin types (even some of those from the mid-to-late 1800s) in everyday circulation. Many of the

coins that granddaddy acquired at face value during that time are probably worth a premium today, even if it is only a few dollars. And if granddaddy was a serious coin collector buying rare coins from dealers and auction houses in the years leading up to 1965, it is possible that the coins he acquired could now be worth considerable money.

2. Post-1965: The federal government's decision to remove silver from circulation in 1965 heightened interest in old coins among the contemporary public. Many people who were not previously collectors started searching through pocket change looking for old coins. Within several years time old coins were rarely seen in everyday use, thus reducing the chances of someone finding a valuable coin in circulation during the 1970s, 1980s, 1990s and into the 21st century. And although people still continue to find very valuable coins in circulation on occasion (a cousin of mine who lives in Connecticut actually received a 1922 No D Lincoln Cent in change in late 2008—the coin is valued at more than $1,000), such finds have always been few and very far between.

Many people who started searching through pocket change beginning in the mid 1960s developed into serious collectors, helping the market to mature and driving prices of many old coins to higher levels. This was a two-edged sword, at least until the advent of third-party certification in the mid 1980s. Granddaddy could have still done very well if he was a serious buyer from dealers and auctions beginning in the late 1960s, but the meteoric rise in popularity of coin collecting also led to the proliferation of counterfeit, altered and just plain overvalued coins in the market. Again, it helps to consider the source for granddaddy's coins when estimating value even within the context of the time frame in which he made most of his acquisitions.

## *How did Granddaddy Preserve the Coins?*

Even if granddaddy did not leave any information about when and where he acquired the coins, the manner in which he preserved them over the years can serve as an important clue to their approximate value. Consider these possibilities:

1. The Sock Drawer: If you found granddaddy's coins rattling around at the bottom of his sock drawer, a cigar box and/ or jumbled together in a plastic bag, it is likely that he acquired the coins either at face value or at an extremely small premium. In other words, he probably knew or suspected that the coins were not worth very much, thus explaining why he did not take any steps to ensure that they would retain their value.

2. Safe Deposit Box or Home Safe: If granddaddy took steps to ensure that the coins were protected against theft by storing them in a safe deposit box or home safe, he obviously knew or suspected that they were worth at least somewhat of a premium. Once again, however, it is important to consider how the coins are stored even within the safe deposit box. Rattling around at the bottom of the safe versus stored in sonically sealed plastic holders for protection convey two radically different clues as to how granddaddy valued the coins.

3. Coin Holders and Albums: If granddaddy stored his coins in specialized holders or albums, then he obviously had an interest in assembling some kind of collection and, as such, took some steps toward preserving the coins. Holders such as these are not a good indicator of current market value, however, as I have seen coins come out of old collector albums that range in price from a few dollars to several thousand dollars.

4. Mint Packaging, Bank-Wrapped Rolls and Other Original Holders: Such storage mediums usually provide considerable protection for the coins that they contain, and the holders themselves are sometimes worth considerable money. As

with basic coin holders and albums, however, coins that granddaddy kept stored in original packaging and similar storage mediums can range in value from a few dollars to several thousand.

5.  Sonically Sealed Plastic Holders: These holders, commonly referred to as "slabs" by professional numismatists and collectors, provide the most secure protection for rare coins from the environment in which they are being stored. The most common "slabs" in the U.S. rare coin market of the 21st century are those from independent third-party certification services such as PCGS and NGC. These "slabs" also provide the firm's opinion of the coin's authenticity and grade. Since the certification process requires an outlay of financial resources, granddaddy probably knew or suspected that his coins were worth enough of a premium to justify paying the certification costs. Or he may have purchased the coins after they had already been certified—either way certified coins have the greatest potential for being worth considerable money, especially if the certification service is one of the more reputable firms such as PCGS and NGC.

*Note: Please see "Chapter XIV: Appraisals and Third-Party Certification" for a detailed description of third-party certification as it pertains to the rare coin market of the 21st century.*

# Chapter XI
# Coins Worth Face Value

Although no one wants to consider this possibility, there is always the chance that some of granddaddy's coins might not be worth more than face value. Of course, modern Cents, Nickels, Dimes and Quarters that are seen in circulation everyday are only worth face value—with the exception of a few extraordinary cases of Mint errors and similar rarities. There are other types of coins that are not seen in daily commerce that granddaddy might have set aside as novelty items but that are still worth only face value. Such pieces actually abound in personal stashes of coins because of the mistaken belief that, because the coins are either not seen in general circulation or are older than most other pieces encountered in everyday use, they must be rare and valuable.

The following chart provides a listing of those coins that granddaddy may have saved but that are worth no more than face value. In each instance, the individual coins in question are assumed to be in average worn condition and were retrieved from circulation at some point in time. Top-quality examples, pieces housed in original U.S. Mint holders or bank-wrapped rolls and coins that were struck in precious metal and/or with a special finish for sale to collectors are not included on this list. Special examples such as those almost always carry somewhat of a premium and must be distinguished from their circulating counterparts.

## Coins Worth Face Value

| Coin Type | Date(s) | Value |
|---|---|---|
| Lincoln Bicentennial Cent | 2009 | Face Value ($0.01) |
| Jefferson Nickel | 1938-1965, Most Issues | Face Value ($0.05) |
| Westward Journey Jefferson Nickel | 2004-2006 | Face Value ($0.05) |
| Bicentennial Washington Quarter | Dual Dated 1776-1976 | Face Value ($0.25) |

| Coin Type | Date(s) | Value |
|---|---|---|
| Statehood Quarters | 1999-2008 | Face Value ($0.25) |
| U.S. Territories Quarters | 2009 | Face Value ($0.25) |
| National Parks Quarters | 2010-2021 | Face Value ($0.25) |
| Kennedy Half Dollar (Copper-Nickel Clad Only) | 1971-Date | Face Value ($0.50) |
| Eisenhower Dollar | 1971-1978 | Face Value ($1.00) |
| Anthony Dollar | 1979-1999 | Face Value ($1.00) |
| Sacagawea Dollar | 2000-Date | Face Value ($1.00) |
| Presidential Dollars | 2007-2016 | Face Value ($1.00) |

# Chapter XII
# Coins with Minimal Value

In most instances, the majority of granddaddy's coins are likely to fall into this category. These are pieces that command a premium above face value but, based on my definition of the term "minimal value," are still worth no more than $100. Most coins in this category were acquired from circulation prior to 1965 or were purchased from local dealers, auctions and flea markets. Many coins and coin sets that granddaddy purchased directly from the United States Mint might also fall into this category, particularly those dated 1960 and later.

Many of granddaddy's coins that have only minimal value are likely to be silver Nickels, Dimes, Quarters and Half Dollars that he retrieved from circulation before or immediately after the federal government announced its decision to cease production of silver coins for commercial use. He may also have obtained most or all of his Morgan and Peace Silver Dollars at this time, although such pieces did not actively circulate and were usually acquired from banks, casinos or dealers.

The following chart provides a listing of those coins that granddaddy may have saved but that command only a modest premium above face value. Most of the coins in this group are assumed to be in average worn condition and were retrieved either from circulation, from local dealers and similar venues or directly from the United States Mint beginning in the early 1960s. High-quality examples with no wear and key-date coins that enjoy strong collector demand are not included on this list as many such pieces carry significant premiums.

## Coins with Minimal Value[1]

| Coin Type | Date(s) | Value[2] |
|---|---|---|
| Indian Cent | 1859-1909, Most Issues | $1.00-$5.00 |
| Lincoln Cent, Wheat Ears Reverse | 1909-1958, Most Issues | $0.02-$1.00 |

| Coin Type | Date(s) | Value[2] |
|---|---|---|
| Buffalo Nickel | 1913-1938, Many Issues | $1.00-$20.00[3] |
| Jefferson Nickel, Wartime Silver Alloy | 1942-1945 | $0.10-$2.50[4] |
| Mercury Dime | 1916-1945, Most Issues | $1.00-$10.00[4] |
| Roosevelt Dime, Silver | 1946-1964 | $0.20-$1.25[4] |
| Standing Liberty Quarter | 1916-1930, Many Issues | $3.00-$20.00[3] |
| Washington Quarter, Silver | 1932-1964, Most Issues | $0.50-$5.00[4] |
| Walking Liberty Half Dollar | 1916-1947, Many Issues | $4.00-$10.00[4] |
| Franklin Half Dollar | 1948-1963 | $3.50-$10.00[4] |
| Kennedy Half Dollar, Silver | 1964 | $3.00-$5.00[4] |
| Kennedy Half Dollar, Silver Clad | 1965-1970 | $1.00-$2.50[4] |
| Morgan Silver Dollar | 1878-1921, Many Issues | $12.00-$20.00[4] |
| Peace Silver Dollar | 1921-1935, Many Issues | $10.00-$20.00[4] |
| Eisenhower Dollar, Proof and Mint State Examples | 1971-1978 | $3.00-$30.00 |
| Anthony Dollar, Proof and Mint State Examples | 1979-1999 | $1.50-$10.00 |
| Sacagawea Dollar, Proof and Mint State Examples | 2000-Date | $1.50-$10.00 |
| Presidential Dollars, Proof and Mint State Examples | 2007-2016 | $1.50-$10.00 |
| Modern U.S. Commemorative Coins, Copper-Nickel Clad and Silver | 1982-Date | $5.00-$100.00 |
| Modern U.S. Proof Sets | 1961-Date | $7.50-$20.00 |
| Special Mint Sets | 1965-1967 | $10.00-$20.00 |
| Modern U.S. Mint Sets | 1969-Date | $7.50-$20.00 |
| Silver American Eagle Bullion Coins | 1986-Date, Most Issues | $15.00-$50.00 |

1=In the context of this chart, I have chosen to define the term "minimal value" as referring to coins that carry a premium above face value but that are still worth no more than $100.

2=Values are approximate and are representative of the most common coins within each given category as defined by type and dates.

3=Examples on which the date is completely worn away are valued lower.

4=Values for many coins in this category will fluctuate with the prevailing spot price of silver.

# Chapter XIII
# Coins with Potentially
# Significant Value

Even within the context of the most commonly encountered United States coins in granddaddy's sock drawer or cigar box, the possibility exists that there will be a rare, important and valuable piece. It is this potential that is probably your greatest motivation for buying this book to help you identify and value the coins that have come into your possession.

There are many coins that granddaddy could have acquired that might have significant value, and the actual value of such pieces could vary widely from a few hundred dollars to several thousand dollars or more. As such, I can only provide you with a list of those specific coins that should be the real target of your search as you work through the identification and valuation process.

As you peruse the list in the following chart and compare it to granddaddy's coins, there are several points to bear in mind. First, I have chosen to define the term "significant value" in this context as referring to coins that are worth more than $100. Second, many of the coins on this list have significant value only in higher grades. Well worn examples might have only minimal value. Third, high-grade examples of even the most common coins often have significant value. For this reason, I have limited this chart to include only those coins that have significant value even in average worn condition.

Fourth, even high-grade examples of valuable coins will be worth much less than reported prices if they have been cleaned, polished, buffed, damaged, repaired or otherwise impaired. Fifth, because of their significant value, many of the coins on this list have long been the subject of counterfeiters. It is especially important that you re-read "Chapter VIII: Counterfeit and Altered Coins" if you believe that you have found a potentially valuable coin. Finally, if you believe you have found a very valuable piece among granddaddy's coins, it is imperative that you solicit the advice of a reputable dealer or auctioneer who can confirm your finding and provide you with an honest and accurate assessment of the coin's true value. Chapters XVI and XVII in this book will provide you with the requisite tools to find a reputable rare coin dealer or auction house.

## *Coins with Potentially Significant Value*[1]

| Coin Type | Dates to Look For[2,3] |
|---|---|
| Indian Cent | 1869; 1870; 1871; 1872; 1877[4]; 1909-S[4] |
| Lincoln Cent | 1909-S V.D.B.[4]; 1909-S; 1914-D[4]; 1922 No D[4]; 1943 Copper[4]; 1943-D Copper[4]; 1943-S Copper[4]; 1955 Doubled Die[4] |
| Buffalo Nickel | 1913-D Type II; 1913-S Type II; 1914-D; 1915-S; 1919-D; 1919-S; 1921-S; 1924-S; 1926-S; 1937-D 3-Legged[4] |
| Mercury Dime | 1916-D[4]; 1921[4]; 1921-D[4]; 1942/1[4]; 1942/1-D[4] |
| Standing Liberty Quarter | 1916[4]; 1919-D; 1919-S; 1921; 1923-S; 1927-S |
| Washington Quarter | 1932-D[4]; 1932-S[4] |
| Walking Liberty Half Dollar | 1916; 1916-D; 1916-S; 1917-D Obverse Mintmark; 1917-D Reverse Mintmark; 1917-S Obverse Mintmark[4]; 1919; 1919-D; 1919-S; 1921[4]; 1921-D[4]; 1921-S[4]; 1938-D |
| Morgan Silver Dollar | 1879-CC; 1880-CC; 1881-CC; 1882-CC; 1883-CC; 1884-CC; 1885-CC; 1888-S; 1889-CC; 1890-CC; 1891-CC; 1892-CC; 1892-S; 1893; 1893-CC; 1893-O; 1893-S[4]; 1894; 1895 (all genuine pieces are proofs); 1895-O; 1895-S; 1899; 1903-O; 1903-S; 1904-S |
| GSA Morgan Silver Dollars | Most Dates |
| Peace Silver Dollar | 1921; 1928[4]; 1934-S[4] |
| Modern U.S. Commemorative Coins, Gold | 1983-Date |

| Coin Type | Dates to Look For[2,3] |
|-----------|------------------------|
| Modern U.S. Proof Sets | 1936; 1937; 1938; 1939; 1940; 1941; 1942; 1950; 1951; 1952; 1953; 1954; 1955; 1968-S with No S Dime; 1970-S with No S Dime; 1971-S with No S Nickel; 1975-S with No S Dime; 1983-S with No S Dime; 1990-S with No S Cent; 1996-S Prestige Set; 1999-S Silver Nine-Piece Set; 2001-S Silver 10-Piece Set |
| Modern U.S. Mint Sets | 1947; 1948; 1949; 1951; 1952; 1953; 1954; 1955; 1956; 1957; 1958 |
| Silver American Eagle Bullion Coins | 1993-P; 1994-P; 1995-P; 1995-W; 1996-P; 1997-P; 2006-W Burnished; 2006-P Reverse Proof |
| Gold American Eagle Bullion Coins | 1986-Date |
| American Buffalo Gold Bullion Coins | 2006-Date |
| First Spouse $10 Gold Bullion Coins | 2007-2016 |
| Platinum American Eagle Bullion Coins | 1997-Date |

1=In this context of this chart, I have chosen to define the term "significant value" as referring to coins that are worth more than $100.

2=High-grade examples of even many common coins have significant value. The coins listed in this chart are those that have significant value even in average worn condition.

3=This chart includes only widely known varieties and Mint errors such as the 1955 Doubled Die Lincoln Cent and 1937-D 3-Legged Buffalo Nickel. Numerous other varieties exist that are still worth considerable money to specialized collectors even though they are not well known among the general public.

4=Beware of counterfeits and altered pieces; see Chapter VIII in this book for more information.

# Chapter XIV
# Appraisals and
# Third-Party Certification

Appraisals and third-party certification provide similar services in that they can both give a definitive opinion regarding the identity and authenticity of granddaddy's coins. Where the two services differ, however, is in the area of valuation. By definition, a properly executed appraisal will provide you an expert's opinion of the value of granddaddy's coins. Third-party certification only provides clues—albeit critical ones—to the price that you should expect to receive when selling coins either outright or through auction. Both services have their merits, but both also have significant drawbacks that you will need to weigh before deciding whether an appraisal or third-party certification is appropriate for granddaddy's coins.

## Definitions

An **appraisal** is both the act of providing a valuation and what the valuation of property by an authorized individual is. The individual providing the appraisal should be an expert in their field.

**Third-party certification** as it applies to the numismatic market of the 21$^{st}$ century is the act of submitting a coin to an independent firm to obtain its opinion of the coin's identity, authenticity and level of preservation. As of this writing, there are several third-party certification services active in the U.S. rare coin market, but I would only recommend two services as being the most reputable and widely accepted among collectors, dealers and other professionals: Professional Coin Grading Service (PCGS) and Numismatic Guaranty Corporation (NGC).

Founded in 1986 and 1987, respectively, PCGS and NGC revolutionized the rare coin industry. Coins submitted to these services are evaluated by teams of professional numismatic graders and authenticators. Pieces that are determined to be genuine, unaltered and problem-free for their respective level of preservation are assigned a numeric grade on a 1-70 scale. The coins are then sonically sealed in tamper-evident plastic holders with a paper insert that lists the date, denomination, grade, variety (if applicable) and a unique barcode for identification purposes. Once certified by PCGS or NGC, a coin carries a grade that can help to determine the price that it will bring when bought and sold in the market. PCGS and NGC-certified coins enjoy universal acceptance, and they also have a high level of liquidity due to the strong reputations that these firms enjoy. In short, PCGS and NGC are the standards for the rare coin industry of the 21$^{st}$ century. They provide a measure of confidence for both novice and veteran collectors when trading in a dynamic market.

## Benefits and Drawbacks

The primary benefit of having some or all of granddaddy's coins appraised or certified has already been stated, but it bears repeating since it is of paramount importance to whether one of these services are appropriate for you. **Both an appraisal and third-party certification (if rendered by reputable individuals or firms) provide a definitive opinion regarding the identity and authenticity of a coin. Each type of service also provides another benefit that has already been addressed: an opinion of a coin's value or important clues that can help determine the value that a coin will bring when offered for sale**. Appraisals and third-party certification, therefore, are critical for some or all of granddaddy's coins that are either known or suspected of having significant value. Only such services will provide you with a fair and impartial assessment of the authenticity and value of granddaddy's coins.

**Certification has one significant advantage over appraisals: coins that have been certified by reputable firms such as PCGS and NGC are usually easier and faster to sell than uncertified coins, and they almost always command stronger prices from the buyer**. Another advantage of third-party certification is that the tamper-evident holders used by PCGS and NGC provide the best storage for valuable coins. Submitting coins to these services, therefore, might be a wise move even if you do not plan on selling in the near future.

Nothing in life is free, however, and appraisals and third-party certification almost always carry with them costs in time and money. These are the potential drawbacks of these services, especially the monetary costs that they involve. I stress the word "potential" in this context, however, since any of granddaddy's coins with significant value will certainly justify the costs of receiving a professional appraisal or submitting them for third-party certification. If granddaddy's coins are worth face value or have only minimal value (especially if they are worth $20 or less), I do not believe that the costs involved with an appraised or third-party certification are justified. My reasoning here is that it does not make sense financially for you to spend, say, $20 plus shipping costs to have a Mercury Dime worth $2.00 certified. You need to be able to recoup your appraisal and/or certification costs if and when you decide to sell, which is certainly not possible if the coin itself is worth less than what you paid for these services.

Third-party certification carries with it one other drawback, and that is the fact that it will not provide you with a definite value for your coins. Rather, third-party certification provides only clues as to the coin's value in the form of authenticity, identity and level of preservation. You will have to conduct additional research either using a price guide or in consultation with a reputable dealer or auctioneer in order to determine approximately what you could expect to receive if and when you decide to sell certified coins.

## Finding a Professional Appraiser

If granddaddy's coins are of sufficient value to justify this service, or if you need to have them appraised in order to positively determine their authenticity or value, you will of course need to find someone who can render a professional appraisal. Very few individuals are dedicated coin appraisers, however, and even many insurance companies that I have contacted over the years do not maintain working relationships with rare coin experts. Most individuals who are qualified to provide a professional appraisal of rare coins are dealers, auctioneers or other industry professionals.

There are many possible ways to find a reputable dealer or auctioneer for United States coins. Chartered by Congress in 1891, the American Numismatic Association (ANA) is the leading hobby organization in U.S. numismatics. The association's website, www.money.org, maintains a searchable database of member dealers and auctioneers. Another excellent source is the Professional Numismatists Guild (PNG), an organization of rare coin and paper money experts whose members are held to high standards of integrity and professionalism. Members of the PNG can be found at the organization's website, www.pngdealers.com. Both the ANA and the PNG are non-profit organizations.

## Submitting Coins for Certification

If you need or choose to submit some of granddaddy's coins to a third-party certification service for authentication and grading, you may experience some difficulty. Reputable third-party certification services such as PCGS and NGC do not accept coin submissions from anyone. Rather, these two firms will only accept submissions from authorized dealers or from members of special hobby organizations such as the PCGS Collectors Club, NGC Collectors Society and the ANA. If you are not a member of such an organization, you will need to find a PCGS and/or NGC authorized dealer in your area who can submit the coins on your behalf. To do so, visit the PCGS and NGC websites at www.pcgs.com and www.ngccoin.com, respectively.

## Approximate Costs

The costs associated with having granddaddy's coins appraised or certified vary depending upon the types of coins involved, the exact service that you require and the appraiser/certification service with which you choose to work. The greatest variation in cost is associated with appraisals. Many dealers and auction houses actually offer free appraisals in the hopes of winning your confidence as a client. I would be wary of such appraisals from dealers, however, as the "values" that they are likely to return under such circumstances are actually the prices that they would like to pay for granddaddy's coins and not necessarily what the coins are truly worth. In order to obtain a more honest appraisal from a dealer, you should expect to pay some sort of fee for the service. Costs will vary, as stated above, and they can be tabulated either by the coin or by the hour.

Free appraisals from auction houses are very attractive offers, inasmuch as auction houses typically derive their revenue by taking a percentage of the price that coins sell for through their auctions. In other words, the more money granddaddy's coins sell for, the more money both you and the auctioneer will be able to put into your pockets. Due to the manner in which they derive revenue, auction houses are almost always motivated to give you more accurate appraisals of what you can expect granddaddy's coin to sell for when they are offered for sale.

Contrary to appraisals, fees associated with third-party certification are easier to pinpoint. As of early 2009, PCGS and NGC submissions will cost you a minimum of $10-$20 per coin, and it could cost as much as several hundred dollars per coin depending upon the type of piece you are submitting, the level of service required for the certification and the turnaround time. To the baseline costs of the submissions you should expect to add shipping and insurance costs, and the submitting dealer might also charge a small fee for facilitating the submission. To find information about current PCGS and NGC certification services and pricing tiers, visit the firms' websites at www.pcgs.com and www.ngccoin.com, respectively.

## *Appraisals and Third-Party Certification*

1. Both an appraisal and third-party certification (if rendered by reputable individuals or firms) provide a definitive opinion regarding the identity and authenticity of a coin.

2. Each type of service also provides expert opinions of a coin's value or important clues that can help determine the value that a coin will bring when offered for sale.

3. Certification has one significant advantage over appraisals: coins that have been certified by reputable firms such as PCGS and NGC are usually easier and faster to sell than uncertified coins, and they almost always command stronger prices from the buyer.

# BRINGING IT ALL TOGETHER

# Expanding Your Coin List

We have come to another section of this book, in the process of identifying and valuing granddaddy's coins, where you should pause to organize the information that you have gathered. It is time to return to the list of coins that you have started building and add a few more columns to incorporate additional information about granddaddy's coins.

Having just presented chapters regarding grading, valuation and third-party certification, I recommend adding three additional columns to your chart to incorporate this information. Remember to use a grading guide such as *The Official American Numismatic Association Grading Standards for United States Coins* by Kenneth Bressett (editor) to determine your coins grades and the indispensible reference *A Guide Book of United States Coins* by R.S. Yeoman to obtain approximate values for the coins. Using my sample list as a guide, and assuming that you are using the 2010 (63rd) edition of the *Guide Book*, your list of granddaddy's coins should now be organized as follows on the next page.

World coins such as the 1895 Great Britain Penny are not listed in the *Guide Book* and will require a specialized reference or consultation with an expert in order to determine value. The same can also be said for the 1930-S Indian Eagle graded MS-64 by PCGS since the *Guide Book* does not provide a value for this coin above the MS-63 grade level.

I have included the three additional columns to our sample list on the following page:

## List of Granddaddy Glynn's Coins[1]

| Country | Denomination | Type | Date | Mintmark | Grade | Certification Service | Estimated Value |
|---|---|---|---|---|---|---|---|
| United States | Cent | Indian | 1902 | None | VG-8 | None | $3 |
| United States | Dime | Seated Liberty | 1843 | O | AU-50 | NGC | $5,000 |
| United States | Half Dollar | Kennedy | 1996 | D | AU-50 | None | Face Value ($0.50) |
| United States | Silver Dollar | Morgan | 1880 | None | VF-20 | None | $22 |
| United States | Eagle-$10 Gold | Indian | 1930 | S | MS-64 | PCGS | N/A (MS-63 Value is $36,500) |
| United States | (5) Coins | Proof Set | 1986 | S | Proof | None | $7 |
| Great Britain | Penny | Queen Victoria | 1895 | None | VF-20 | None | -- |

1=Prepared June-December 2009, by Jeff Ambio.

# PART FIVE

# SELLING GRANDDADDY'S COINS

# Chapter XV
# General Considerations

Now that you have positively identified granddaddy's coins and acquired more-or-less accurate estimates of their worth, the time has come for you to decide what to do with the inheritance or gift that you have received. If some or all of granddaddy's coins are worth of least a small premium face value, and if you do not see yourself developing into an avid collector, you will probably want to consider selling the coins. Many people approach this process with a certain amount of fear and trepidation, usually because selling coins is a foreign concept with which they have no practical experience. This need not be the case, however, as selling coins can be an enjoyable and rewarding experience, especially when all you have left to do at the end of the process is cash the check you receive! The purpose of this section is to familiarize you with the basics of selling coins in the U.S. numismatic market of the 21st century and to equip you with the tools you need to make the process as effortless and lucrative as possible.

## *General Considerations*

1. Once you understand the basics and are equipped with the proper tools, selling coins can be an enjoyable, rewarding and lucrative experience.

# Chapter XVI
# Selling Coins to a Dealer

Perhaps the most obvious way to liquidate granddaddy's coins is to sell them to a dealer who specializes in coins. Not all of granddaddy's coins might be suitable for this kind of sale, however, and there are also other factors for you to consider that will help ensure that you get the most money when the time comes to sell. Let's take a close look at the "ins and outs" of selling granddaddy's coin to a dealer.

## *Benefits and Drawbacks*

**Selling to a dealer is usually the easiest and quickest way to liquidate granddaddy's coins**. For small to moderate-size holdings, transactions can usually be completed within an hour or two, and many dealers will not require you to make an appointment (although it usually helps) before you visit their place of business. This gives you the flexibility to work the sale of granddaddy's coins into your schedule. Selling to a dealer also places the check into your hands immediately with no need to worry about waiting 30-45 days (the usual settlement period for major rare coin auction houses). Finally, **dealers are often able to pay you more money for certain types of coins than you would receive if you placed those pieces into auction**. See page 107 for a list of those types of coins that I believe are best sold outright to a dealer.

There are drawbacks to selling granddaddy's coins to a dealer, however, and you must weigh these carefully against the real or perceived benefits. Unlike auction houses, dealers are in the business of reselling coins, which means that their primary motivation is usually to purchase coins at the lowest possible prices so as to make the most profit when they go to sell. While I cannot deny the time, value of money, and the benefit of receiving payment as soon as possible, it is likely that you will just not get the most money when selling certain types of coins to a dealer. Remember also that a dealer is just one person or, at most, they represent one company.

Unless you shop around and receive buy offers from other dealers, the dealer with which you are doing business will not be making their bid in a competitive environment. A lack of significant competition is another factor that could cause you to leave a lot of money on the table when selling granddaddy's coins to a dealer.

## Finding a Reputable Coin Dealer

If you decide that selling to a dealer is the best way to liquidate granddaddy's coins, it should be relatively easy for you to find an honest, reputable firm with which to do business. **Of particular importance during this stage of the selling process is your insistence on finding a dealer who is a member of a recognized and prestigious professional or hobby organization**. Both the American Numismatic Association (ANA) and the Professional Numismatists Guild (PNG) maintain databases of member dealers on their websites www.money.org and www.pngdealers.com, respectively. These databases are searchable by state, allowing you to find a dealer within your area. The ANA and PNG hold their members to high standards of professionalism and integrity, and both organizations also offer arbitration services to settle disputes between dealers and clients that might arise during the process of doing business. To guarantee that you receive the utmost in customer service and the fairest prices when selling granddaddy's coins, insist on choosing a dealer that is an ANA and/or PNG member.

An excellent way to find and visit with multiple dealers simultaneously is to attend a local, regional or national coin show or convention. Such gatherings are held every month in different parts of the country, and the largest ones attract hundreds of dealers who specialize in all types of United States and foreign coins. The ANA and PNG offer information on some of the most important coin shows held each year, while the Internet and newspapers are the best sources for finding local and regional conventions in your area.

What if there are no ANA or PNG member dealers close to where you live? What if there are no coin shows or conventions scheduled to take place in your area? Should you consider selling to a local dealer who is not a member of such an organization? In my opinion, you should still insist on doing business with an ANA and/or PNG member. There is nothing to fear from shipping granddaddy's coins to a dealer who is located far from where you live so long as you are dealing with a reputable firm and you follow some simple guidelines. These are discussed below.

## The Process: What to Expect

As already stated, selling coins to a dealer is usually an easy process. There are only a few steps that you need to follow to complete the process as quickly and enjoyably as possible.

1. <u>Find More Than One Reputable Dealer</u>: Plan on finding at least two different dealers so as to solicit multiple buy offers before you decide upon a specific individual or firm with which to do business. It is always a good idea to shop around.

2. <u>Contact Each Dealer Via Telephone</u>: You should next contact each dealer via telephone before visiting their place of business. Get acquainted with each dealer before showing them granddaddy's coins so that you can verify their credentials, their place of business and the hours during which they conduct business. Telephone calls also provide you with the opportunity to give the dealer an idea of the types of coins you have and how many pieces you are interested in selling. This will save you time and effort since many dealers specialize in certain areas of numismatics and might not be able to make competitive buy offers for some or all of granddaddy's coins. For example, a dealer that specializes in world coins would probably not be a realistic option if granddaddy left you only United States coins.

   Additionally, many dealers travel to local, regional and national coin shows and conventions, so they may not always be available at their established place of business even during published business hours. Conversely, the dealer will be able to tell you if and when they will be traveling to a coin show in your area, which might provide you with the opportunity to meet face-to-face and further discuss selling granddaddy's coins. Bear in mind also that if granddaddy's coins are of sufficient value most dealers will be willing to make a special trip to your home, bank or place of work for the express purpose of making the purchase.

Another way to save time and hassle when selling granddaddy's coins is to send a list of granddaddy's coins to the dealer before making an appointment to visit with them. This will allow the dealer to determine what you have beforehand so that they can decide whether or not they are even interested in purchasing coins of these types. Use the list that you have built to satisfy this requirement, but be sure to remove estimated values as well as other appraisals/ buy offers from the list so as not to prejudice the dealer before they have a chance to evaluate your coins.

3. <u>Make an Appointment</u>: Many dealers do not require you to set an appointment prior to visiting their place of business, especially those that advertise heavily on the Internet or in local publications. Even so, I believe that it is a good idea to set an appointment so that you can expect to have the dealer's undivided attention when you arrive with granddaddy's coins. If you have not done so already, now is the perfect time to give the dealer an idea of the types of coins you have and how many pieces you are interested in selling. This gives them the opportunity to gather the resources they need to evaluate the coins before you arrive, thus saving you both time and making the process more relaxing for everyone involved.

4. <u>Plan to Spend at Least One Hour with Each Dealer</u>: When setting an appointment with a dealer or otherwise deciding to visit their place of business with granddaddy's coins in tow, plan on spending at least an hour. Dealers will need to carefully evaluate every piece in order to ensure proper identification and valuation, so be careful not to rush them lest they make critical mistakes that could cost you money. If you plan on spending some time with dealers while they are

evaluating granddaddy's coins you will also find that most are very willing to talk with you about the coins, the hobby of coin collecting and other types of coins that they might be selling. This is a great way to learn more about granddaddy's coins and perhaps gain an insight into a hobby and market in which you might not have had much experience.

> *I distinctly remember one unfortunate seller who visited a dealership in Texas with many coins to sell. The seller did not plan his day properly and left inadequate time for the dealer to evaluate and value his coins. After only a portion of the coins had been properly evaluated, the seller became impatient and requested that the dealer speed the process along. The dealer complied, came up with a total dollar amount for the seller's coins, gave him a check and sent him on his way. Several days later, when the dealer had more time to evaluate the coins he had just purchased, he discovered that one of the Buffalo Nickels for which he had paid only a few dollars was an example of a very rare variety. The dealer subsequently sold the coin for more than $100,000—money that I am sure the original seller could have used. (The other lesson from this example, of course, is the importance of properly evaluating and valuing granddaddy's coins before you contact dealers with the intent to sell.)*

5. Receive Payment: The selling process obviously ends when both you and the dealer agree upon the prices to be paid for each of the coins that you are offering. Expect to be paid with a check drawn on a business account, although you might be able to receive cash for smaller sales. If you need access to the cash embodied in a check as quickly as possible, the dealer should also be willing to direct you to their bank where you can cash the check right away.

> *When I was younger I used to conduct a considerable amount of business with a very nice dealer in New*

*Jersey. He never kept much cash in his store for security reasons, so when I sold him coins he always paid me with a check. Without me even asking, he always directed me to his bank (which happened to be right across the street!) and told me that I could cash the check right away if I needed immediate access to the money. The dealer's checks were always good, his bank was fast and courteous and the entire selling process was very rewarding for me.*

6. <u>Shipping Granddaddy's Coins to a Dealer</u>: If you are unable to find an ANA or PNG member dealer in your area, or if one will not be traveling to your area for a convention, you should seriously consider shipping granddaddy's coins to a reputable firm that will provide you with a fair assessment of value and the best prices possible. Do not be afraid to do this—remember, ANA and PNG member dealers are held to high standards of professionalism and integrity, and their organizations offer arbitration services to settle difference between dealers and clients. Just follow these simple steps and you should have little reason to fret:

   i. <u>Contact the Dealer Beforehand</u>: I know this sounds obvious, but I have worked as a professional numismatist long enough to recall several incidents when packages of coins simply arrived at an office without prior warning or supporting paperwork. Get in contact with the dealer first, verify their credentials, discuss the shipping, evaluation and buying processes with them and make sure they know to look for your package. Don't forget to ask the dealer for recommendations on how to properly pack the coins and what other types of shipping materials they recommend for safety and security. And if you do not accept the dealer's purchase offer, find out beforehand who pays the cost of shipping the coins back to you.

   ii. <u>Make an Inventory List of Granddaddy's Coins</u>: If you have not already made a list of granddaddy's coins, make sure you do so before shipping the coins to a dealer. It might also be a good idea to take pictures or scans of the more expensive pieces. The extra time and effort up front will save you immeasurably if the coins are lost in the mail or a dispute arises with the dealer.

   iii. <u>Use the United States Post Office's Insured Registered Mail Service</u>: In my experience, this is the safest way to ship coins and other valuables through the mail. On a recent trip to my local Post Office branch, several of the employees told me that the Hope Diamond was shipped through the Post Office using Insured Registered Mail. If that service is deemed safe enough to ship a world-renowned treasure, it should be more than adequate to ship granddaddy's coins. Insured Registered Mail is not the fastest way to ship but each postal worker who handles the shipment is required to sign for the package, thus insuring maximum security.

iv. Save all Shipping Materials: Keep your shipping register and tracking numbers handy to follow the package as it moves through the postal system and, eventually, is received and signed for by the dealer.

7. Remember Safety and Security: Whether you are taking granddaddy's coins to a dealer's place of business or to your local Post Office, always remember simple safety and security practices. Do not carry the coins in the open where everyone can see the valuables that you are transporting. Even a simple duffle bag or backpack is sufficient to conceal granddaddy's coins from prying eyes. And do not tell anyone you do not know or trust what you are carrying or where you are going.

## Potential Pitfalls

I have already addressed several possible mistakes that you could make when selling granddaddy's coins to a dealer, such as selling to a dealer who is not a member of an organization such as the ANA or PNG and failing to solicit more than one purchase offer before you decide to make the sale. There is one other potential pitfall that could cost you hundreds if not thousands of dollars when selling granddaddy coins. **DO NOT sell granddaddy's coins to a local jeweler, pawnbroker or any other type of dealership that does not specialize in rare coins**. Jewelers and pawnbrokers often dabble in rare coins, but they are not their primary business. Often, such "coin dealers" are only really interested in the precious metal content of the coins and have neither knowledge nor interest in the considerable collectible value of the coins. Find a dedicated coin dealer and make sure they are a member of a leading hobby or industry organization such as the ANA and PNG.

## *Types of Coins that are Best Sold to Dealers*

As previously stated, there are certain types of coins that you would be much better off selling to a dealer than placing in an auction. Often these are coins with minimal collectible value, coins that have not been certified by a service such as PCGS or NGC and/ or coins whose value is derived exclusively from the precious metal that they contain. For lists of values to use in qualifying grand-daddy's coins for possible sale to a dealer, see the pricing charts in Chapters XI-XIII of this book. Bear in mind, of course, that you could also do very well selling extremely rare and valuable coins to a dealer. This is especially true if you can find a dealer who specializes in the types of coins that you are trying to sell. Often such dealers are "market makers" in their area(s) of specialization, which allows them to establish prices for extremely important coins and provides them with access to the leading collectors and investors who are seeking such pieces.

# Selling Coins to a Dealer

1.  Selling to a dealer is usually the easiest and quickest way to liquidate granddaddy's coins.

2.  Dealers are often able to pay you more money for certain types of coins than you would receive if you placed those pieces into auction.

3.  Insist on finding a dealer who is a member of a recognized and prestigious professional or hobby organization such as the American Numismatic Association (ANA) and/or the Professional Numismatists Guild (PNG).

4.  DO NOT sell granddaddy's coins to a local jeweler, pawn-broker or any other type of dealership that does not specialize in rare coins.

# Chapter XVII
# Selling Coins Through Auction

Selling coins through auction is a longer, more involved process than selling coins to a dealer. The reward is often worth the extra effort, however, as certain types of coins need to sell in the competitive environment of a major numismatic auction in order to guarantee that they bring the highest prices possible.

## Benefits and Drawbacks

**The primary benefit of selling coins through auction is that it places the coins before a large number of potential buyers and, in so doing, creates a highly competitive environment.** Of particular importance here is the inclusion of BOTH dealers and collectors among the potential buyers. Unlike dealers who can only pay so much for a coin because they are constrained by the need to make a profit when reselling, collectors are often willing to pay more to get the pieces they need to complete their collections. As such, **auctions can often provide you with greater returns when selling certain types of coins**.

As with dealers, of course, auctions also have some drawbacks for sellers. The most significant of these is the amount of time that you will need to wait in order to receive your check. The time between the actual sale of the coins and your receipt of the check—known in the auction community as the settlement period—varies considerably depending upon the type of auction through which you are selling. The longest settlement periods in the rare coin auction industry of which I am aware last five-to-six weeks. There are ways to make the reality of a settlement period more palatable, such as with cash advances drawn off the estimated proceeds of the auction sale. If you need immediate access to 100% of the money embodied in the sale of granddaddy's coins, however, the auction process might not be for you.

Auctioneers also charge a seller's commission, which is a percentage of the (hammer) price that the coins bring at auction.

Unlike a buyer's premium, the seller's commission is assessed on the seller, which means that it comes out of the check that you will be receiving for the sale of granddaddy's coins. If the auctioneer does their job properly in marketing the coins and generating sufficient bidder interest, the higher prices generated often make the seller's commission more than worth it in the eyes of the seller. You must be careful, however, to select both the right auctioneer and the proper types of coins for the auction process lest the seller's commission becomes a burden. In other words, if not approached properly and conducted wisely, the auction process can net you less funds than you would receive had you chosen to sell granddaddy's coins to a dealer.

Another potential drawback of the auction process is that it may seem foreign or complex to many sellers. At its foundation, selling coins to a dealer is no more complex than selling any other type of commodity. Goods change hands, money changes hands and the transaction ends. There is no middleman as involved with an auction sale, and no need to understand terminology such as settlement period, hammer price and buyer's premium.

The auction process need not be frightening, however, and it is actually easy to understand and can be as effortless as walking a coin into a dealer's shop to sell over the counter. I urge you to learn about the basic steps involved in selling coins through auction since doing so will enable you to get the highest prices possible when selling each one of granddaddy's coins. Let's take a closer look at the auction process.

## *Finding a Reputable Auctioneer*

Reputable auction houses that specialize in United States coins can be found in much the same way as reputable dealers. **I urge you to find an auctioneer that is a member of (or whose owners/ principals are members of) a prestigious professional or hobby organization such as the American Numismatic Association (ANA) and/or the Professional Numismatists Guild (PNG)**. Visit the organizations' websites at www.money.org and www.pngdealers.com, respectively, for lists of recommended auctioneers.

## The Process: What to Expect

Once you have located one or more auctioneers, you are ready to begin the auction process in earnest.

1. <u>Find More than One Reputable Auctioneer</u>: Since you are going to be negotiating a seller's commission with the auctioneer, it is a good idea to contact multiple auction houses so that you can compare rates and select the most advantageous commission. Additionally, auctioneers conduct their sales on different schedules. The first auctioneer you contact might not be holding another sale for several months, while the second might be accepting consignments for an auction to be held within the next couple of weeks. How quickly you need to receive payment might also play a part in choosing between two or more auction houses.

2. <u>Contact Each Auctioneer Via Telephone</u>: Even more so than when conducting business with dealers, it is imperative that you contact each potential auctioneer for granddaddy's coins via telephone. Many times this step is a necessity since there are far fewer reputable auctioneers for United States coins than there are dealers. There is a high probability that you will not live near enough to a major numismatic auction house to visit in person. Since shipping granddaddy's coins to an auction house is also probably going to be a necessity, preliminary telephone calls will be required to set up all of the details of the transaction and prepare the auctioneer to receive the coins. And of course, time spent on the phone early on will help the auctioneer qualify the coins for consignment and provide both parties with the opportunity to negotiate the seller's commission and other details. Sending the auctioneer a copy of your coin list will also save time here, but be sure to remove any estimated values or other appraisals/buy offers so as not to prejudice the auctioneer before they see your coins.

   *As amazing as it might seem, I can recall a situation while working for a major numismatic auctioneer when a package of coins arrived in the mail quite un-*

*expectedly. The person who sent the coins had not called anyone at the auction house prior to placing the package in the mail, nor had they included important contact information such as their name (!), telephone number or even a return address. The auction house had no other choice but to place the package in their vault and wait for the sender to call in and inquire as to the whereabouts and status of their consignment. Failure to follow proper procedure in this instance created considerable confusion and resulted in the seller having to wait even longer to receive the proceeds of their auction sale.*

3.  <u>Scheduling a Visit from the Auctioneer</u>: Many times auctioneers will travel to your home, bank or place of business to evaluate the coins and pick them up for auction. The coins will have to meet certain prerequisites for value to warrant this treatment, of course, but it never hurts for you to ask the auctioneer if they would be willing to provide you with this service.

4.  <u>Shipping Granddaddy's Coins to an Auctioneer</u>: Whether you hand deliver them yourself, have the auctioneer pick them up at your home or place of business or ship them via the United States Post Office, rest assured that you are going to have to get granddaddy's coins to the auction house in order for them to be placed into a sale. Reputable auctioneers will not place material into their sales without taking physical possession. The auction house must be able to examine the material so as to make accurate statements of authenticity and quality to prospective bidders, and they must also be able to guarantee to their bidders that once winning bids are placed and the invoices are paid, the lots will be available for immediate release. It is also important to remember that, just as dealers need to see coins firsthand before making a competitive offer, auctioneers will need to inspect the coins in person in order to determine their suitability for auction. The procedures for shipping

coins to a an auctioneer are the same as those outlined above for shipping coins to a dealer, but I have chosen to list them again here (in condensed format) for the convenience of the reader.

5. <u>Contact the Auctioneer Beforehand</u>: Once again, make sure the auctioneer and their staff know that the coins are coming, the contents of the package(s) and approximately when to expect the shipment. Don't forget to ask the auctioneer for recommendations on how to properly pack the coins and what other types of shipping materials they recommend for safety and security.

   i. <u>Make an Inventory List of Granddaddy's Coins</u>: If you have not already made a list of granddaddy's coins, make sure you do so before shipping the coins to an auctioneer. It might also be a good idea to take pictures or scans of the more expensive pieces. The extra time and effort up front will save you immeasurably if the coins are lost in the mail or a dispute arises with the auction house.

   ii. <u>Use the United States Post Office's Insured Registered Mail Service</u>: In my experience, this is the safest way to ship coins and other valuables through the mail.

   iii. <u>Save all Shipping Materials</u>: Keep your shipping register and tracking numbers handy to follow the package as it moves through the postal system and, eventually, is received and signed for by the auctioneer.

   iv. <u>Remember Safety and Security</u>: When traveling to and from the post office, remember simple safety and security procedures such as concealing the coins from general view and keeping your travel schedule and route confidential.

*I remember a telephone conversation that I had with a potential consignor while working for a major rare coin auction house in California. After qualifying* the gentleman's consignment and agreeing upon a seller's commission, he seemed willing to go ahead with the auction sale of his coins. When I began to explain the necessity of shipping his coins and detailing the shipping process, I was met with a comment along the lines of, "If you expect me to ship you the coins you must assume I am the dumbest person on the planet." He then hung up on me without uttering another word. Make sure you know how the auction process works so as to save both time and effort for everyone involved.

6. Negotiating Your Seller's Commission: Once the auctioneer has verified the types and quantity of coins that you will be consigning, you can start to negotiate a seller's commission. The total value of your consignment will determine how much you can negotiate on this point. Standard seller's commissions are often in the range of 10-20%, but if you have a particularly valuable and/or important consignment you should be able to negotiate for a much lower consignment rate in the range of 0-5%.

    *(Note: Remember that most auctioneers assess sellers' commissions on the hammer price of the lots, not the realized price. The realized price includes the buyer's premium, and it is usually the price that the auctioneer uses in post-sale reporting.)*

7. Completing the Necessary Paperwork: Selling coins through auction requires that you complete a considerable amount of paperwork, so be prepared to devote some time to this part of the process. If your auctioneer is experienced and professional, they should make every effort to make this part of the process as smooth and effortless as possible. Expect to complete at least the following two forms:

    i.  Schedule of Consigned Items: A listing of all of the coins that you are consigning.

    ii. Consignment Agreement: The contract between you and the auctioneer to sell the coins. Among other things, the consignment agreement will contain your seller's commission.

8. <u>Minimum Bids and Reserves</u>: Since you remain the rightful owner of your coins all the way up until the point in time when the auctioneer drops the gavel, you retain the right to place minimum bids and reserves. The auctioneer cannot prevent you from doing this, but you must remember two points. First, reserves need to be placed with the auctioneer before the auction commences. Do not attempt to bid on your own coins during the auction. Second, auctioneers will often charge you a fee for those coins that do not meet your minimum bid or reserve. This fee, called a buyback fee, minimum bid fee or reserve fee, can be steep—expect a number in the range of 10-20% of the reserve amount.

9. <u>Watching Your Coins Sell</u>: Once you have negotiated your rates and completed all of the paperwork, there is nothing left to do but wait for the auction to open and watch your coins sell. The auctioneer will handle all other considerations such as cataloging, imaging and marketing. Due to the time required to execute these important tasks, remember that it might be several weeks or months from the time you consign your coins to the time that the auction is actually held.

10. <u>Receive Payment</u>: Once the auction closes you and the auctioneer will enter the settlement period—the time that you must wait before the auctioneer releases the funds from your auction sales. Depending upon the type of auction through which you are selling, settlement periods can vary from a few days to more than a month.

## *Potential Pitfalls*

Insist upon auctioning granddaddy's coins through an auctioneer that is a member of a recognized hobby or professional organization such as the ANA and/or PNG. Correspondingly, **DO NOT auction granddaddy's coins through an auction house that does not specialize in rare coins**. It is perfectly acceptable to use an auctioneer that sells a wide variety of collectible material such as stamps and firearms, but make sure that they have dedicated sales for rare coins and that they are widely known in the numismatic market. Auction houses that do not have such credentials will not be able to attract the serious bidders that you need to deliver the strongest possible prices for granddaddy's coins.

## Types of Coins that are Best Sold through Auction

Rare coin auction houses of the 21st century have become so experienced and diversified that they now offer numerous different venues geared toward maximizing profit on a wide variety of coins. Even so, there are certain types of coins that tend to do best in auction, as well as other types that are still probably best sold outright to a dealer. Coins with significant value and/or whose value is based on the collectibles market (i.e., not the precious metals market) tend to garner more money at auction than if they were sold directly to a dealer. Coins that have already been certified by PCGS and NGC are best consigned to an auctioneer since such pieces usually have sufficient value to have justified granddaddy paying the certification fees. Additionally, esoteric pieces that cater to a highly specialized segment of the rare coin market should be consigned to an auction to give them a better chance of finding an elusive buyer.

I do not recommend auctioning coins with minimal value (less than $100) or whose value is derived almost exclusively from their precious metal content. Inexpensive coins are often grouped together for auction sales, with the result that the individual coins in the grouping tend to bring less than what they would have realized had they been offered for individual sale. And coins that are worth little more than melt value are likely to sell for similar amounts of money either to dealers or through auction. Why pay the auctioneer a seller's commission out of that amount when you could have put more money into your pocket by selling the coin directly to a dealer?

## *Selling Coins through Auction*

1. The primary benefit of selling coins through auction is that it places the coins before a large number of potential buyers and, in so doing, creates a highly competitive environment.

2. Auctions can often provide with greater returns when selling certain types of coins than if you had chosen to sell the coins outright to a dealer.

3. Insist on finding an auctioneer that is a member of (or whose owners/principals are members of) a prestigious professional or hobby organization such as the American Numismatic Association (ANA) and/or the Professional Numismatists Guild (PNG).

4. DO NOT auction granddaddy's coins through an auction house that does not specialize in rare coins.

# Selling Coins Through Auction

# Chapter XVIII
# When Selling is Not an Option

For some readers, there may be circumstances in which you cannot or do not want to sell some or all of granddaddy's coins. If this is the case, you need not fear: there are still ways in which you can derive benefit from the coins that granddaddy left behind.

## *Spending (Yes, Spending) Granddaddy's Coins*

If you have followed the steps for identification and valuation presented in this book, you may have discovered that some or all of granddaddy's coins are worth only face value. You obviously cannot sell such coins to a dealer or place them on consignment with an auction house. If the money that these coins represent is more important to you than their value as keepsakes, there is no reason why you cannot simply spend the coins. Of course, you must be completely certain that the coins that you are spending really do not carry an extra premium either as collectibles or due to their precious metal content. If you are unsure of a coin's true value, I recommend taking it to a reputable dealer or auctioneer who can tell you for certain what the coin is worth. The worst that could happen is for the dealer or auctioneer to chuckle a little when they tell you that granddaddy's Quarter is worth only twenty-five cents.

## *Giving Granddaddy's Coins Away*

Giving away some or all of granddaddy's coins is another way to derive pleasure and benefit from pieces that are worth only face value. Perhaps granddaddy saved some coins such as Bicentennial Washington Quarters and Eisenhower Dollars that you do not see in everyday use. Instead of just spending the coins, you might want to consider giving them as gifts to children, grandchildren or other family members. This is a great way to use granddaddy's coins as gifts or for educational purposes while still keeping them in the family. And who knows, you might spark an interest in someone else that could blossom into a lifetime of collecting coins.

Many coins with minimal value also make great gifts for family and friends. Common-date Morgan and Peace Silver Dollars in worn condition are usually worth no more than $20, yet they hold considerable appeal as collectibles and keepsakes. These are old, large-size coins with plenty of history and nearly an ounce of silver. Such pieces make excellent gifts for children and grandchildren at birthdays, holidays and special events.

## Keeping Granddaddy's Coins

Regardless of whether they are worth face value or hundreds of thousands of dollars, there are certainly good reasons for wanting to keep granddaddy's coins for yourself. Perhaps after reading this book you have developed an interest in coin collecting. Granddaddy's coins would certainly serve as the basis for your own collection.

On the other hand, coin collecting as a hobby might not appeal to you in the slightest. Even if this is the case, you still might want to think twice before selling, spending or making gifts of granddaddy's coins. The sentimental value of these family heirlooms might be such that you would like to keep them, perhaps as a tribute to granddaddy and a reminder of his achievement in finding and saving these coins. If so, be sure to follow my advice in Chapter IV and elsewhere in this book for safeguarding granddaddy's coins for the benefit of future generations. And as much as I would appreciate the revenue from additional book sales, make sure that you record all of the identification and valuation information that you have learned about granddaddy's coins while using this book. After all, you would not want your heirs scratching their heads one day and wondering what to do with granddaddy's coins.

# BRINGING IT ALL TOGETHER

# Completing Your Coin List

If you have made the decision to sell some or all of granddaddy's coins, and if you have begun to contact dealers and/or auctioneers with the intention of doing so, you will have gathered the final bit of information required to complete your coin list. This information is the buy offer/appraisal of each of granddaddy's coins made by the dealers/auctioneers. I recommend including this valuable information in your list, but only for use by you or someone you trust in disposing of granddaddy's coins. Be sure to remove this information from the list before showing it to other dealers and/or auctioneers so as not to prejudice their opinion of your coins.

Assuming that I have shown the "coins" on my sample list to one dealer and one auctioneer, the completed version of my list would look like the one on the following page.

Bear in mind that some dealers/auctioneers might now have an interest in purchasing/auctioning certain types of coins, either because they do not deal in those types of coins or because the coins do not carry a premium above face value. Also, when obtaining appraisal values from auctioneers, be sure to clarify whether the value they are providing is what they expect the coin to bring at auction or what they expect you to receive for the coin in your settlement check (i.e., after deduction of pertinent grading fees, seller's commissions or other costs).

I have included the last two columns to our sample list on the following page:

# List of Granddaddy Glynn's Coins[1]

| Country | Denom-ination | Type | Date | Mint-mark | Grade | Certification Service | Estimated Value | Dealer #1 Buy Offer | Auctioneer #1 Appraisal |
|---|---|---|---|---|---|---|---|---|---|
| United States | Cent | Indian | 1902 | None | VG-8 | None | $3 | $1.50 | -- |
| United States | Dime | Seated Liberty | 1843 | O | AU-50 | NGC | $5,000 | $3,750 | $4,500 |
| United States | Half Dollar | Kennedy | 1996 | D | AU-50 | None | Face Value ($0.50) | -- | |
| United States | Silver Dollar | Morgan | 1880 | None | VF-20 | None | $22 | $15 | -- |
| United States | Eagle-$10 Gold | Indian | 1930 | S | MS-64 | PCGS | N/A (MS-63 Value is $36,500) | $35,000 | $40,000 |
| United States | (5) Coins | Proof Set | 1986 | S | Proof | None | $7 | -- | -- |
| Great Britain | Penny | Queen Victoria | 1895 | None | VF-20 | None | -- | $1 | -- |

1=Prepared June-December 2009, by Jeff Ambio.

# APPENDICES

# Appendix A
## Tools of the Trade Checklist

| | Recommended Supplies | Estimated Cost |
|---|---|---|
| | **A Guide Book of United States Coins** (*The Official Red Book*) by R.S. Yeoman | $10-$20 |
| | **The Official American Numismatic Association Grading Standards for United States Coins** by Kenneth Bressett OR **Photograde—Official Photographic Grading Guide for United States Coins** by James F. Ruddy | $10-$20 |
| | Non-Vinyl Flip-Type Coin Holders | <$1/Holder |
| | A Soft, Nonabrasive Material Such as Velvet Fabric | <$5/Yard |


| | Optional Supplies | Estimated Cost |
|---|---|---|
| | **Standard Catalog of World Coins** by Colin R. Bruce (senior editor), multiple volumes | $35-$65+/ vol. |
| | Flip-Open Loupe with 10X Magnification | $20-$50+ |

# Appendix B
## Useful Websites

This list is by no means exhaustive, but it does provide you with a few of the more widely used websites for obtaining information and supplies useful in identifying, valuing and selling rare coins.

### Leading Hobby/Industry Organizations

**American Numismatic Association (ANA)**
Internet Address: www.money.org
Toll Free: (800) 367-9723

**Professional Numismatists Guild (PNG)**
Internet Address: www.pngdealers.com

### Leading Coin Supply Houses

**CoinSupplyExpress.com**
Internet Address: www.coinsupplyexpress.com
Toll Free: (800) 503-6461

**CollecTons**
Internet Address: www.collectons.com
Toll Free: (866) 680-2655

**Amazon.com**
(Books Only)
Internet Address: www.amazon.com

### Third-Party Certification Services

**Professional Coin Grading Service (PCGS)**
Internet Address: www.pcgs.com
Toll Free: (800) 447-8848

**Numismatic Guaranty Corporation (NGC)**
Internet Address: www.ngccoin.com
Toll Free: (800) NGC-COIN

# Appendix C
# General Grading Guidelines for United States Coins

What follows are general verbal descriptions for each major tier on the numeric grading scale for United States coins. While I have provided images of Morgan Silver Dollars to illustrate the general characteristics of each tier, there is no substitute for acquiring a reference book that deals specifically with grading United States coins. Only by using a specialized grading guide can you obtain detailed descriptions and specific images for a wide variety of United States coins.

## Mint State

**Abbreviation:** MS
**Corresponding Numbers on the 1-70 Grading Scale:** 60-70
**General Description:** A coin that was made for, but has not seen commercial use.

Morgan Dollar
Mint State, Obverse

Morgan Dollar
Mint State, Reverse

## About Uncirculated

**Abbreviation:** AU
**Corresponding Numbers on the 1-70 Grading Scale:** 50, 53, 55, 58
**General Description:** A coin that retains virtually all of the original detail.

Morgan Dollar
About Uncirculated, Obverse

Morgan Dollar
About Uncirculated, Reverse

### Extremely Fine

**Abbreviation:** EF
**Corresponding Numbers on the 1-70 Grading Scale:** 40, 45
**General Description:** A coin that retains much of the original detail.

Morgan Dollar
Extremely Fine, Obverse

Morgan Dollar
Extremely Fine, Reverse

### Very Fine

**Abbreviation:** VF
**Corresponding Numbers on the 1-70 Grading Scale:** 20, 25, 30, 35
**General Description:** A coin that retains approximately half of the original detail.

Morgan Dollar
Very Fine, Obverse

Morgan Dollar
Very Fine, Reverse

### Fine

**Abbreviation:** F
**Corresponding Numbers on the 1-70 Grading Scale:** 12, 15
**General Description:** A coin with somewhat less than half of the original detail remaining.

Morgan Dollar
Fine, Obverse

Morgan Dollar
Fine, Reverse

### Very Good

**Abbreviation:** VG
**Corresponding Numbers on the 1-70 Grading Scale:** 8, 10
**General Description:** A coin with a small amount of detail remaining.

Morgan Dollar
Very Good, Obverse

Morgan Dollar
Very Good, Reverse

## Good

**Abbreviation**: G
**Corresponding Numbers on the 1-70 Grading Scale:** 4, 6
**General Description:** A coin with minimal detail remaining.

Morgan Dollar
Good, Obverse

Morgan Dollar
Good, Reverse

## About Good

**Abbreviation**: AG
**Corresponding Numbers on the 1-70 Grading Scale:** 3
**General Description:** A coin with such little detail remaining that even the rims are mostly smooth.

Morgan Dollar
About Good, Obverse

Morgan Dollar
About Good, Reverse

## Fair

**Abbreviation**: FR
**Corresponding Numbers on the 1-70 Grading Scale:** 2
**General Description:** Hardly any detail remaining.

Morgan Dollar
Fair, Obverse

Morgan Dollar
Fair, Reverse

## Poor

**Abbreviation**: PO
**Corresponding Numbers on the 1-70 Grading Scale:** 1
**General Description:** A coin with virtually no detail remaining; one that is barely identifiable.

Morgan Dollar
Poor, Obverse

Morgan Dollar
Poor, Reverse

# Appendix D
# Values of Frequently Encountered United States Coins

| Coin Type | Years Issued | Value[1] | Dates to Look For[2,3] |
|---|---|---|---|
| Indian Cent | 1859-1909 | $1.00-$5.00 | 1869; 1870; 1871; 1872; 1877[4]; 1909-S[4] |
| Lincoln Cent, Wheat Ears Reverse | 1909-1958 | $0.02-$1.00 | 1909-S V.D.B.[4]; 1909-S; 1914-D[4]; 1922 No D[4]; 1943 Copper[4]; 1943-D Copper[4]; 1943-S Copper[4]; 1955 Doubled Die[4] |
| Lincoln Bicentennial Cent | 2009 | Face Value ($0.01) | -- |
| Buffalo Nickel | 1913-1938 | $1.00-$20.00[5] | 1913-D Type II; 1913-S Type II; 1914-D; 1915-S; 1919-D; 1919-S; 1921-S; 1924-S; 1926-S; 1937-D 3-Legged[4] |
| Jefferson Nickel, Nickel Composition | 1938-1942; 1946-Date | Face Value ($0.05) | -- |
| Jefferson Nickel, Wartime Silver Alloy | 1942-1945 | $0.25-$2.50[6] | -- |
| Westward Journey Jefferson Nickel | 2004-2006 | Face Value ($0.05) | -- |
| Mercury Dime | 1916-1945 | $1.00-$10.00[6] | 1916-D[4]; 1921[4]; 1921-D[4]; 1942/1[4]; 1942/1-D[4] |
| Roosevelt Dime, Silver | 1946-1964 | $0.75-$1.25[6] | -- |

| Coin Type | Years Issued | Value[1] | Dates to Look For[2,3] |
|---|---|---|---|
| Standing Liberty Quarter | 1916-1930 | $3.00-$20.00[5] | 1916[4]; 1919-D; 1919-S; 1921; 1923-S; 1927-S |
| Washington Quarter, Silver | 1932-1964 | $2.00-$5.00[6] | 1932-D[4]; 1932-S[4] |
| Bicentennial Washington Quarter | Dual-Dated 1776-1976 | Face Value ($0.25) | -- |
| Statehood Quarters | 1999-2008 | Face Value ($0.25) | -- |
| U.S. Territories Quarters | 2009 | Face Value ($0.25) | -- |
| American's Beautiful National Parks Quarters | 2010-2020 | Face Value ($0.25) | -- |
| Walking Liberty Half Dollar | 1916-1947 | $5.00-$10.00[6] | 1916; 1916-D; 1916-S; 1917-D Obverse Mintmark; 1917-D Reverse Mintmark; 1917-S Obverse Mintmark[4]; 1919; 1919-D; 1919-S; 1921[4]; 1921-D[4]; 1921-S[4]; 1938-D |
| Franklin Half Dollar | 1948-1963 | $5.00-$10.00[6] | -- |
| Kennedy Half Dollar, Silver | 1964 | $4.00-$5.00[6] | -- |
| Kennedy Half Dollar, Silver Clad | 1965-1970 | $1.50-$2.50[6] | -- |
| Kennedy Half Dollar, Copper-Nickel Clad | 1971-Date | Face Value ($0.50) | -- |

| Coin Type | Years Issued | Value[1] | Dates to Look For[2,3] |
|---|---|---|---|
| Morgan Silver Dollar | 1878-1921 | $12.00-$20.00[6] | 1878-CC; 1879-CC; 1880-CC; 1881-CC; 1882-CC; 1883-CC; 1884-CC; 1885-CC; 1888-S; 1889-CC; 1890-CC; 1891-CC; 1892-CC; 1892-S; 1893; 1893-CC; 1893-O; 1893-S[4]; 1894; 1895 (all genuine pieces are proofs); 1895-O; 1895-S; 1899; 1903-O; 1903-S; 1904-S |
| Peace Silver Dollar | 1921-1935 | $10.00-$20.00[6] | 1921; 1928[4]; 1934-S[4] |
| Eisenhower Dollar | 1971-1978 | Face Value ($1.00) | -- |
| Anthony Dollar | 1979-1999 | Face Value ($1.00) | -- |
| Sacagawea Dollar | 2000-Date | Face Value ($1.00) | -- |
| Presidential Dollars | 2007-2016 | Face Value ($1.00) | -- |

1=Values are approximate and are representative of the most common examples of each coin type in average worn condition.

2=High-grade examples of even many common coins have significant value. The coins listed in this column are those that have significant value even in average worn condition.

3=This chart includes only widely known varieties and Mint errors such as the 1955 Doubled Die Lincoln Cent and 1937-D 3-Legged Buffalo Nickel. Numerous other varieties exist that are still worth considerable money to specialized collectors even though they are not well known among the general public.

4=Beware of counterfeit and altered pieces; see Chapter VIII in this book for more information.

5=Examples on which the date is completely worn away are valued lower.

6=Values for many coins in this category will vary depending upon the spot of silver.

# Appendix E
# United States Paper Money

As the title makes clear, the primary subject of this book is coins. Even so, I would be remiss if I did not make mention of some commonly encountered types of United States paper money, especially since it is entirely possible that granddaddy might also have some of these pieces in his sock drawer or cigar box with his coins.

The following images and fact lists are designed to help you identify these widely encountered paper money types and focus on key features for valuation purposes. I have also provided approximate value estimates for the *most commonly encountered examples* of each note type in average worn condition. As with United States coins, even the most common United States paper money types and dates can bring significant premiums at high levels of preservation. Additionally, there are many rare dates, errors, etc. among United States paper money that command significant premiums. To obtain more accurate pricing data for these and other paper money types, I suggest acquiring one of two reference books: **Paper Money of the United States** (various editions available) by Arthur L. and Ira S. Friedberg or **A Guide Book of United States Paper Money** (*The Official Red Book*) also by Arthur L. and Ira S. Friedberg.

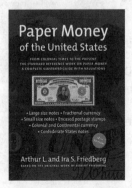 

Above left: *Paper Money of the Unites States* by Arthur L. and Ira S. Friedberg
Above right: *A Guide Book of United States Paper Money* (*The Official Red Book*)
also by Arthur L. and Ira S. Friedberg

## *Small Size $1 Legal Tender Note*

**Date(s):** 1928

**Key Identifying Features:** Red seal on the front of the note to the left of Washington's portrait; inscription UNITED STATES NOTE on the front of the note above the portrait

**Special Considerations:** N/A

**Approx. Value for the Most Common Examples of the Type:** $50.00-$100.00

Small Size $1 Legal Tender Note, Front

Small Size $1 Legal Tender Note, Back

## *Small Size $1 Silver Certificate*

**Date(s):** 1928-1957

**Key Identifying Features:** Blue seal on the front of the note; inscription SILVER CERTIFICATE on the front of the note above the portrait

**Special Considerations:** Notes of this type vary in design and placement of the blue seal.

**Approx. Value for the Most Common Examples of the Type:** $1.50-$5.00

Small Size $1 Silver Certificate, Front

Small Size $1 Silver Certificate, Back

## *Small Size $1 Federal Reserve Note*

**Date(s):** 1963-Date

**Key Identifying Features:** Green seal on the front of the note to the right of Washington's portrait; inscription FEDERAL RESERVE NOTE on the front of the note above the portrait

**Special Considerations:** The later dates of this type are the current circulating $1 notes of the United States.

**Approx. Value for the Most Common Examples of the Type:** Face Value ($1.00)

Small Size $1 Federal Reserve Note, Front

Small Size $1 Federal Reserve Note, Back

## World War II Emergency Issue $1 Note—Hawaii

**Date(s):** 1935

**Key Identifying Features:** Inscription HA-WAII on both sides of the note; Brown seal on the front of the note to the right of Washington's portrait

**Special Considerations:** These 1935-dated $1 Silver Certificates were issued for use in Hawaii after the attack on Pearl Harbor.

**Approx. Value for the Most Common Examples of the Type:** $20.00-$50.00

WWII Emergency Issue $1 Note—Hawaii, Front

WWII Emergency Issue $1 Note—Hawaii, Back

## World War II Emergency Issue $1 Note—Europe and North Africa

**Date(s):** 1935

**Key Identifying Features:** Yellow seal on the front of the note to the right of Washington's portrait

**Special Considerations:** These 1935-dated $1 Silver Certificates were issued for use with the Armed Forces in Europe and North Africa.

**Approx. Value for the Most Common Examples of the Type:** $20.00-$50.00

WWII Emergency Issue $1 Note— Europe and North Africa, Front

WWII Emergency Issue $1 Note— Europe and North Africa, Back

## Small Size $2 Legal Tender Note

**Date(s):** 1928-1963

**Key Identifying Features:** Red seal on the front of the note to the right of Jefferson's portrait; inscription UNITED STATES NOTE on the front of the note above the portrait; portrait of Jefferson's home Monticello on the back of the note

**Special Considerations:** N/A

**Approx. Value for the Most Common Examples of the Type:** $3.00-$10.00

Small Size $2 Legal Tender Note, Front

Small Size $2 Legal Tender Note, Back

## Small Size $2 Federal Reserve Note

**Date(s):** 1976-2003

**Key Identifying Features:** Green seal on the front of the note to the right of Jefferson's portrait; inscription FEDERAL RESERVE NOTE on the front of the note above the portrait

**Special Considerations:** The later dates of this type are the current circulating $2 notes of the United States, although such pieces are seldom encountered in everyday use. Most $2 bills are obtainable only from banks or directly from the Treasury Department.

**Approx. Value for the Most Common Examples of the Type:** Face Value ($2.00)

Small Size $2 Federal Reserve Note, Front

Small Size $2 Federal Reserve Note, Back

## Small Size $5 Legal Tender Note

**Date(s):** 1928-1963

**Key Identifying Features:** Red seal on the front of the note to the left of Lincoln's portrait; inscription UNITED STATES NOTE on the front of the note above the portrait

**Special Considerations:** N/A

**Approx. Value for the Most Common Examples of the Type:** $7.50-$15.00

Small Size $5 Legal Tender Note, Front

Small Size $5 Legal Tender Note, Back

## Small Size $5 Silver Certificate

**Date(s):** 1934-1953

**Key Identifying Features:** Blue seal on the front of the note to the right of Lincoln's portrait; inscription SILVER CERTIFICATE on the front of the note above the portrait

**Special Considerations:** N/A

**Approx. Value for the Most Common Examples of the Type:** $7.50-$15.00

Small Size $5 Silver Certificate, Front

Small Size $5 Silver Certificate, Back

## Small Size $5 Federal Reserve Bank Note

**Date(s):** 1929
**Key Identifying Features:** Brown seal on the front of the note to the right of Lincoln's portrait; inscription NATIONAL CURRENCY on the front of the note above the portrait
**Special Considerations:** N/A
**Approx. Value for the Most Common Examples of the Type:** $20.00-$50.00

Small Size $5 Federal Reserve Bank Note, Front

Small Size $5 Federal Reserve Bank Note, Back

## Small Size $5 Federal Reserve Note

**Date(s):** 1928-Date
**Key Identifying Features:** Green seal on the front of the note to the right of Lincoln's portrait; inscription FEDERAL RESERVE NOTE on the front of the note above the portrait
**Special Considerations:** The later dates of this type are the current circulating $5 notes of the United States.
**Approx. Value for the Most Common Examples of the Type:** Face Value ($5.00)

Small Size $5 Federal Reserve Note, Front

Small Size $5 Federal Reserve Note, Back

## World War II Emergency Issue $5 Note—Hawaii

**Date(s):** 1934
**Key Identifying Features:** Inscription HAWAII on both sides of the note; Brown seal on the front of the note to the right of Lincoln's portrait
**Special Considerations:** These 1934-dated $5 Federal Reserve Notes were issued for use in Hawaii after the attack on Pearl Harbor.
**Approx. Value for the Most Common Examples of the Type:** $50.00-$100.00

WWII Emergency Issue $5 Note—Hawaii, Front

WWII Emergency Issue $5 Note—Hawaii, Back

## World War II Emergency Issue $5 Note—Europe and North Africa

**Date(s):** 1934

**Key Identifying Features:** Yellow seal on the front of the note to the right of Lincoln's portrait

**Special Considerations:** These 1934-dated $5 Silver Certificates were issued for use with the Armed Forces in Europe and North Africa.

**Approx. Value for the Most Common Examples of the Type:** $25.00-$75.00

WWII Emergency Issue $5 Note—
Europe and North Africa, Front

WWII Emergency Issue $5 Note—
Europe and North Africa, Back

## Small Size $10 Silver Certificate

**Date(s):** 1933-1953

**Key Identifying Features:** Blue seal on the front of the note; inscription SILVER CERTIFICATE on the front of the note above the portrait

**Special Considerations:** Notes of this type different in the placement of the blue seal.

**Approx. Value for the Most Common Examples of the Type:** $20.00-$50.00

Small Size $10 Silver Certificate, Front

Small Size $10 Silver Certificate, Back

## Small Size $10 Federal Reserve Bank Note

**Date(s):** 1929

**Key Identifying Features:** Brown seal on the front of the note to the right of Hamilton's portrait; inscription NATIONAL CURRENCY on the front of the note above the portrait

**Special Considerations:** N/A

**Approx. Value for the Most Common Examples of the Type:** $20.00-$50.00

Small Size $10 Federal Reserve Bank Note, Front

Small Size $10 Federal Reserve Bank Note, Back

## Small Size $10 Federal Reserve Note

**Date(s):** 1928-Date

**Key Identifying Features:** Green seal on the front of the note to the right of Hamilton's portrait; inscription FEDERAL RESERVE NOTE on the front of the note above the portrait

**Special Considerations:** The later dates of this type are the current circulating $10 notes of the United States.

**Approx. Value for the Most Common Examples of the Type:** Face Value ($10.00)

Small Size $10 Federal Reserve Note, Front

Small Size $10 Federal Reserve Note, Back

## World War II Emergency Issue $10 Note—Hawaii

**Date(s):** 1934

**Key Identifying Features:** Inscription HAWAII on both sides of the note; Brown seal on the front of the note to the right of Hamilton's portrait

**Special Considerations:** These 1934-dated $10 Federal Reserve Notes were issued for use in Hawaii after the attack on Pearl Harbor.

**Approx. Value for the Most Common Examples of the Type:** $50.00-$100.00

WWII Emergency Issue $10 Note—Hawaii, Front

WWII Emergency Issue $10 Note—Hawaii, Back

## World War II Emergency Issue $10 Note—Europe and North Africa

**Date(s):** 1934

**Key Identifying Features:** Yellow seal on the front of the note to the right of Hamilton's portrait

**Special Considerations:** These 1935-dated $1 Silver Certificates were issued for use with the Armed Forces in Europe and North Africa.

**Approx. Value for the Most Common Examples of the Type:** $30.00-$80.00

WWII Emergency Issue $10 Note—
Europe and North Africa, Front

WWII Emergency Issue $10 Note—
Europe and North Africa, Back

## Small Size $10 Gold Certificate

**Date(s):** 1928
**Key Identifying Features:** Gold seal on the front of the note to the right of Hamilton's portrait
**Special Considerations:** N/A
**Approx. Value for the Most Common Examples of the Type:** $75.00-$200.00

Small Size $10 Gold Certificate, Front

Small Size $10 Gold Certificate, Back

## Small Size $20 Federal Reserve Bank Note

**Date(s):** 1929
**Key Identifying Features:** Brown seal on the front of the note to the right of Jackson's portrait; inscription NATIONAL CURRENCY on the front of the note above the portrait
**Special Considerations:** N/A
**Approx. Value for the Most Common Examples of the Type:** $35.00-$75.00

Small Size $20 Federal Reserve Bank Note, Front

Small Size $20 Federal Reserve Bank Note, Back

## Small Size $20 Federal Reserve Note

**Date(s):** 1963-Date
**Key Identifying Features:** Green seal on the front of the note to the right of Jackson's portrait; inscription FEDERAL RESERVE NOTE on the front of the note above the portrait
**Special Considerations:** The later dates of this type are the current circulating $20 notes of the United States.
**Approx. Value for the Most Common Examples of the Type:** Face Value ($20.00)

Small Size $20 Federal Reserve Note, Front

Small Size $20 Federal Reserve Note, Back

## *World War II Emergency Issue $20 Note—Hawaii*

**Date(s):** 1934

**Key Identifying Features:** Inscription HA-WAII on both sides of the note; Brown seal on the front of the note to the right of Jackson's portrait

**Special Considerations:** These 1934-dated $20 Federal Reserve Notes were issued for use in Hawaii after the attack on Pearl Harbor.

**Approx. Value for the Most Common Examples of the Type:** $50.00-$200.00

WWII Emergency Issue $20 Note—Hawaii, Front

WWII Emergency Issue $20 Note—Hawaii, Back

## *Small Size $20 Gold Certificate*

**Date(s):** 1928

**Key Identifying Features:** Gold seal on the front of the note to the right of Jackson's portrait

**Special Considerations:** N/A

**Approx. Value for the Most Common Examples of the Type:** $75.00-$200.00

Small Size $20 Gold Certificate, Front

Small Size $20 Gold Certificate, Back

## *Small Size $50 Federal Reserve Bank Note*

**Date(s):** 1929

**Key Identifying Features:** Brown seal on the front of the note to the right of Grant's portrait; inscription NATIONAL CURRENCY on the front of the note above the portrait

**Special Considerations:** N/A

**Approx. Value for the Most Common Examples of the Type:** $70.00-$100.00

Small Size $50 Federal Reserve Bank Note, Front

Small Size $50 Federal Reserve Bank Note, Back

## Small Size $50 Federal Reserve Note

Small Size $50 Federal Reserve Note, Front

**Date(s):** 1928-Date
**Key Identifying Features:** Green seal on the front of the note to the right of Grant's portrait; inscription FEDERAL RESERVE NOTE on the front of the note above the portrait
**Special Considerations:** The later dates of this type are the current circulating $50 notes of the United States.
**Approx. Value for the Most Common Examples of the Type:** Face Value ($50.00)

Small Size $50 Federal Reserve Note, Back

## Small Size $100 Legal Tender Note

**Date(s):** 1966
**Key Identifying Features:** Red seal on the front of the note to the right of Franklin's portrait; inscription UNITED STATES NOTE on the front of the note above the portrait
**Special Considerations:** N/A
**Approx. Value for the Most Common Examples of the Type:** $125.00-$200.00

Small Size $100 Legal Tender Note, Front

Small Size $100 Legal Tender Note, Back

## Small Size $100 Federal Reserve Bank Note

**Date(s):** 1929
**Key Identifying Features:** Brown seal on the front of the note to the right of Franklin's portrait; inscription NATIONAL CURRENCY on the front of the note above the portrait
**Special Considerations:** N/A
**Approx. Value for the Most Common Examples of the Type:** $125.00-$200.00

Small Size $100 Federal Reserve Bank Note, Front

Small Size $100 Federal Reserve Bank Note, Back

## Small Size $100 Federal Reserve Note

Small Size $100 Federal Reserve Note, Front

**Date(s):** 1928-Date

**Key Identifying Features:** Green seal on the front of the note to the right of Franklin's portrait; inscription FEDERAL RESERVE NOTE on the front of the note above the portrait

**Special Considerations:** The later dates of this type are the current circulating $100 notes of the United States.

Small Size $100 Federal Reserve Note, Back

**Approx. Value for the Most Common Examples of the Type:** Face Value ($100.00)

# Glossary

**About Good:** The descriptive term associated with the numeric designation of 3 on the 70-point grading scale for United States coins. The abbreviation for About Good is AG.

**About Uncirculated:** The descriptive term associated with the numeric designations of 50, 53, 55 and 58 on the 70-point grading scale for United States coins. The abbreviation for About Uncirculated is AU.

**American Numismatic Association:** Chartered by Congress in 1891, the American Numismatic Association is the leading hobby organization in U.S. numismatics. The American Numismatic Association is often referred to by the abbreviation ANA. It is a non-profit organization.

**Bidder:** A participant in an auction who seeks to buy a lot in the sale.

**Brilliant Uncirculated:** The descriptive term that corresponds to the MS-60, MS-61 and MS-62 grade levels. Brilliant Uncirculated is abbreviated as BU.

**Business Strike:** A regular-issue coin struck on normally prepared planchets by dies that are also given normal preparation. Business strikes coins can also be referred to as circulation strikes, and they are coins that the Mint produces for use in commerce.

**Buyback Fee:** In a rare coin auction, the fee that the auctioneer assesses on the consignor when a lot fails to meet its reserve or minimum bid. A Buyback Fee is sometimes referred to as a "Minimum Bid Fee" or "Reserve Fee".

**Buyer's Premium:** In a rare coin auction, the fee that the auctioneer assesses on the buyer when they purchase a lot in the auction. Buyer's premiums are assessed on the hammer price of a lot.

**Cent:** A United States coins with a face value of 1 cent which is often erroneously referred to as a "penny." Cents have been struck in the United States Mint since 1793.

**Certified:** A coin that has been submitted to a third-party grading service and returned to the submitter in a sonically sealed, tamper-evident holder. Coins certified by PCGS and NGC enjoy nearly universal acceptance in the U.S. rare coin market of the early 21st century.

**Choice AU:** The descriptive term that corresponds to the AU-55 and, to a lesser extant, AU-58 grade levels.

**Choice Proof:** Descriptive term that correspond to the Proof-63 and Proof-64 grade levels.

**Choice Uncirculated/Choice Mint State/Choice BU:** Descriptive terms that correspond to the MS-63 and MS-64 grade levels.

**Cleaning:** The use of an abrasive substance or device to alter the surfaces of a coin. Cleaned coins often display numerous scattered hairlines on one or both sides and, as impaired examples, are usually not eligible for certification at the major third-party grading services.

**Commemorative Coin:** A coin struck to honor a person, place or event. Many U.S. Commemoratives were also struck to raise funds for events relating to the theme(s) depicted on the coins.

**Consignor:** A participant in an auction who seeks to sell material through the sale.

**Date:** The numerals on a coin that identify the year in which it was produced. For most United States coins, the date appears either on the obverse at the lower border or in the center of the reverse.

**Denomination:** The monetary value of a coin as assigned by the issuing government. For most United States coins, the denomination is present either at the lower-reverse border or in the center of the reverse. It can be expressed numerically (25 C., 50 C., for example) or in words (TWENTY CENTS, TWENTY D., etc.).

**Design:** The general motif of the coin, to include all markings and features that have been placed upon its surfaces.

**Designer's Initials:** The small letter(s) that identify the artist who is credited with designing a specific coin. Unlike mintmarks (for which they are often mistaken), designer's initials are usually very small, well concealed within the coin's design and may not be readily identifiable as to which letter(s) they represent.

**Device:** An element of a coin's design. In general usage among numismatists, the term "device" usually refers to the artistic elements of a coin's design and does not include such statutory elements such as the date and mintmark. Devices are usually elements such as portraits, eagles, the rays of the sun and wreaths.

**Dime:** A United States coins with a face value of 10 cents. Dimes have been struck in the United States Mint since 1796.

**Edge:** The third side of a coin, and that which separates the obverse and reverse. Common edge types on United States coins are reeded, plain and lettered (with or without ornamental devices).

**Extremely Fine:** The descriptive term associated with the numeric designations of 40 and 45 on the 70-point grading scale for United States coins. Abbreviations for Extremely Fine include EF and XF.

**Fair:** The descriptive term associated with the designation 2 on the 70-point grading scale for United States coins. Fair is sometimes abbreviated as FR.

**Field:** The portion of a coin's design where there are no devices or design elements.

**Fine:** The descriptive term associated with the numeric designations of 12 and 15 on the 70-point grading scale for United States coins. Fine is sometimes abbreviated as F.

**Gem Proof:** The descriptive term that corresponds to the Proof-65 and Proof-66 grade levels. Often times only the word "Gem" is needed to convey the same meaning.

**Gem Uncirculated/Gem Mint State/Gem BU:** The descriptive terms that correspond to the MS-65 and MS-66 grade levels. Often times only the word "Gem" is needed to convey the same meaning.

**Good:** The descriptive term associated with the numeric designations of 4 and 6 on the 70-point grading scale for United States coins. Good is sometimes abbreviated as G.

**Hairlines:** Thin lines on a coin's surfaces that, when use in reference to a business strike example, are indicative of cleaning or another form of mishandling. Hairlines are also used to describe light handling marks on proof coins and, in this case, are not always the result of cleaning. Unlike die polish lines, hairlines are set below the surface of a coin.

**Half Dollar:** A United States coins with a face value of 50 cents. Half Dollars have been struck in the United States Mint since 1795.

**Hammer Price:** In a rare coin auction, the price that a lot sells for at the time that the auctioneer drops the gavel.

**Impaired:** A descriptive term for coins that have been cleaned, damaged, whizzed, repaired or otherwise mishandled to the point where they will trade at a discounted price. It is the stated policy of major third-party grading services such as PCGS and NGC that impaired coins are not eligible for certification and will be returned to the submitter without being mounted in a plastic holder.

**Insert:** The small piece of paper included in the holder with coins certified by PCGS, NGC and other third-party grading services. Upon the insert are found such important information as the coin's date, denomination, grade and, if applicable, variety.

**Legend:** Generally speaking, any inscription that appears on the surface of a coin. Many numismatists use the term "legend" to describe the inscription that identifies the country of origin for a specific coin. For almost all United States coins, the legend appears as UNITED STATES OF AMERICA, and it is usually (but not always!) present at or near the border on the reverse of the coin.

**Lot:** In the rare coin auction market, a unit of sale in an auction. Lots can be comprised of a single item or multiple items.

**Luster:** The original finish imparted to a coin at the time of striking. Or, the amount and intensity of light reflected from the surface of a coin.

**Minimum Bid:** see *Reserve*.

**Minimum Bid Fee:** see *Buyback Fee*.

**Mint State:** A coin struck for circulation that does not display any evidence of wear. Mint State coins are graded on a numeric scale from 60-70. The term "Uncirculated" also describes a Mint State coin.

**Mintmark:** The small letter(s) that identify in which mint a coin was struck.

**Motto:** An inscription that forms part of a coin's design. For United States coins, the term "motto" is often reserved for the inscriptions IN GOD WE TRUST and E PLURIBUS UNUM.

**Near-Gem:** The descriptive term that corresponds to the MS-64 and Proof-64 grade levels.

**Near-Mint:** The descriptive term that corresponds to the AU-58 grade level.

**Nickel:** A United States coins with a face value of 5 cents. Nickel Five-Cent pieces have been struck in the United States Mint since 1866.

**Numismatic Guaranty Corporation:** Founded in 1987, NGC authenticates, grades and encapsulates coins for a fee. Along with PCGS, it is the leading third-party certification service in the U.S. rare coin market of the early 21st century.

**Numismatics:** The study or collection of rare coins. A person who studies, collects or invests in rare coins is known as a numismatist.

**Obverse:** The front, or "heads" side of a coin. For most United States coins, the obverse is the side of the coin that bears the date.

**Quarter:** A United States coins with a face value of 25 cents. Quarters have been struck in the United States Mint since 1796.

**Polishing:** An especially severe form of cleaning. Coins that have been polished display unnaturally bright and/or glossy-textured surfaces. Technically impaired, polished coins are not eligible for certification at the major third-party grading services.

**Poor:** The descriptive term associated with the numeric designation of 1 on the 70-point grading scale for United States coins. Poor is sometimes abbreviated as PO.

**Professional Coin Grading Service:** Founded in 1986, PCGS authenticates, grades and encapsulates coins for a fee. Along with NGC, it is the leading third-party certification service in the U.S. rare coin market of the early 21st century.

**Professional Numismatists Guild:** An organization of rare coin and paper money experts whose members are held to high standards of integrity and professionalism. The abbreviation for the Professional Numismatists Guild is PNG. It is a non-profit organization.

**Proof:** A coin struck with specially prepared dies on a specially prepared planchet. Proof coins are usually struck with two or more blows from the dies, the presses simultaneously operating at slower speeds and higher striking pressures. This extra care is designed to impart uncommonly sharp striking detail to the devices on both sides of the coin. Proof coins are usually not intended for circulation but, rather, are prepared by the Mint for sale to collectors as well as presentation and other special purposes.

*Note: The term Proof is not a grade like Extremely Fine, About Uncirculated or even Mint State. Instead, the term Proof refers to a method of manufacture.*

**Realized Price:** In a rare coin auction, the sum of the hammer price and the buyer's premium.

**Reserve:** In a rare coin auction, the minimum dollar amount that a bidder must be willing to pay in order for a lot to sell. A Reserve can also be referred to as "Minimum Bid".

**Reserve Fee:** see *Buyback Fee.*

**Reverse:** The back, or "tails" side of a coin. For most United States coins, the reverse is the side of the coin that bears the denomination.

**Rim:** The border, often raised, around the obverse and reverse of a coin.

**Seller's Commission:** In a rare coin auction, the fee that the auctioneer assesses on the consignor for offering their material in the auction. Seller's commissions are usually assessed on the hammer price of a lot, not the realized price.

**Settlement Period:** In a rare coin auction, the period of time that elapses between the end of an auction and the consignors' receipt of payment.

**Silver Dollar:** A United States coins with a face value of $1.00. The United States Mint struck Silver Dollars for commercial use from 1794 through 1935. One Dollar coins struck in the United States Mint for commercial use beginning in 1971 are often mistakenly classified as Silver Dollars, although such pieces bear no resemblance to their counterparts from 1878-1935 apart from face value.

**Superb Gem:** The descriptive term that corresponds to the MS-67, MS-68, MS-69, Proof-67, Proof-68 and Proof-69 grade levels.

**Surfaces:** The obverse and reverse of a coin.

**Toning:** The color or colors seen on one or both sides of many coins. The intensity and variety of toning that a coin displays is a function of how, where and how long it was stored.

**Very Fine:** The descriptive term associated with the numeric designations of 20, 25, 30 and 35 on the 70-point grading scale for United States coins. The abbreviation for Very Fine is VF.

**Very Good:** The descriptive term associated with the numeric designations of 8 and 10 on the 70-point grading scale for United States coins. The abbreviation for Very Good is VG.

**Whizzing:** An attempt to simulate original luster on a coin's surface through the use of a wire brush or similar device. Whizzed coins are considered to be impaired and are not eligible for certification at the major third-party grading services.

# Bibliography

Akers, David W. and Ambio, Jeff. *A Handbook of 20th Century United States Gold Coins: 1907-1933, 2nd Edition*. Irvine, California: Zyrus Press, 2008.

Ambio, Jeff. *Collecting & Investing Strategies for Barber Dimes*. Irvine, California: Zyrus Press, 2009.

Ambio, Jeff. *Collecting & Investing Strategies for United States Gold Coins*. Irvine, California: Zyrus Press, 2008.

Ambio, Jeff. *Collecting & Investing Strategies for Walking Liberty Half Dollars*. Irvine, California: Zyrus Press, 2008.

Breen , Walter. *Walter Breen's Complete Encyclopedia of U.S. and Colonial Coins*. New York, New York: Doubleday, 1988.

Breen, Walter. *Walter Breen's Encyclopedia of United States and Colonial Proof Coins: 1722-1977*. New York, New York: FCI Press, Inc., 1977.

Bressett, Kenneth (editor). *The Official American Numismatic Association Grading Standards for United States Coins, 6th Edition*. Atlanta, Georgia: Whitman Publishing, LLC, 2005.

*Coin Dealer Newsletter, The, Vol. XLVII, No. 20*. Torrance, California: May 15, 2009.

*Coin Dealer Newsletter Monthly Supplement, The, Vol. XXXIV, No. 5*. Torrance, California: May 8, 2009.

Dannreuther, John and Garrett, Jeff. *The Official Red Book of Auction Records: 1995-2004, U.S. Small Cents-Silver Dollars*. Atlanta, Georgia: Whitman Publishing, LLC, 2005.

Fivaz, Bill. *United States Gold Counterfeit Detection Guide*. Atlanta, Georgia: Whitman Publishing, LLC, 2005.

Professional Coin Grading Service. *Official Guide to Coin Grading and Counterfeit Detection*. New York, New York: House of Collectibles, 1997.

Ruddy, James F. *Photograde: Official Photographic Grading Guide for United States Coins, 19th Edition*. Irvine, California: Zyrus Press, Inc., 2005.

Yeoman, R. S. *A Guide Book of United States Coins, 63rd Edition*. Atlanta, Georgia: Whitman Publishing, LLC, 2009.